Make Your Next Trade Show Pay... Not Cost!

"Be Outrageously Successful at Exhibiting"

By Troy Milligan

- *Avoid the 3 biggest mistakes made by 87% of all exhibitors.*

- *How to get the best display at the best price using the Internet.*

- *The magic technique that turns any exhibit into a guaranteed profit machine.*

- *Exposing the myths about premiums and giveaways.*

- *Discover the secrets to highly effective 3-second marketing.*

Milligan's Marketing Magic Series Vol. 1

Questions Welcome
Contact Troy Milligan at: www.TroyMilligan.com

Disclaimer: This publication is being distributed with the expressed and implied understanding that the
author and publisher are not engaged in rendering legal, accounting or other professional advice. If legal
advice or other expert assistance is required, the services of a competent professional should be sought.
While the author has made every effort to be factual, and verify the information provided, neither the
author nor the publisher assume any responsibility for errors, inaccuracies or omissions, your results may
vary. Any perceived slights to people, groups, or organizations are completely unintentional.

Note for Librarians: A cataloguing record for this book is available from Library and Archives Canada at
www.collectionscanada.ca/amicus/index-e.html
ISBN 1-4120-8792-9

Offices in Canada, USA, Ireland and UK

Book sales for North America and international:
Trafford Publishing, 6E–2333 Government St.,
Victoria, BC V8T 4P4 CANADA
phone 250 383 6864 (toll-free 1 888 232 4444)
fax 250 383 6804; email to orders@trafford.com
Book sales in Europe:
Trafford Publishing (UK) Limited, 9 Park End Street, 2nd Floor
Oxford, UK OX1 1HH UNITED KINGDOM
phone 44 (0)1865 722 113 (local rate 0845 230 9601)
facsimile 44 (0)1865 722 868; info.uk@trafford.com
Order online at:
trafford.com/06-0548

10 9 8 7 6 5 4

Thanks to those who helped shape my life.

Some Family

My parents who both taught me that success was for those that *keep trying*.

My daughters Alisha and Melanie who, like magic, bring me more joy than I can measure. My sisters Diana and Peggy for donating their sweatshirts so I could make my first strait jacket and learn that *escape is only in the mind*.

Some Friends

Paul Zill, my magical mentor who believed in me way before I could believe in myself. And then we have George Proud, Sam Bailey, Jesse Klosiewicz, Lee Allen, Tex Counts, and my great friend Tim Hall, all master magicians.

Dorothy Young – Houdini's on-stage assistant, who shared her intimate stories of life touring with Harry and Bess during his prime in 1925. Even at age 98, her kindness and talents are inspirational, and you can still see in her eyes, just what Houdini saw: an author, world class ballroom dancer, Broadway star, silent movie actress, nationally acclaimed artist, business woman, philanthropist, and assistant to the Great Houdini.

- Wow, could Houdini pick 'em or what?

Marianne Waterstradt, my magical partner, my best friend, my attorney, my proofreader, and yes my *Dorothy Young*. She is **The Genuine Babe of Babes.** *- Wow, can I pick 'em or what?*

Some Freaks

Melvin Burkhart – **The Human Block Head**, Sealo – **The Seal Boy**, Pricilla – **The Monkey Girl**, her husband Emmett – **The Alligator Skinned Man**, Lester/Ester – **Half Man-Half Woman**, Miss Sandra – **The Albino Sword Swallower**, and Prince Arthur – **The Worlds Smallest Negro Midget**. As my heroes, they graciously accepted me as one of them and taught me that *adversity is just a doorway to opportunity.*

With special thanks to my first love,
my ex-wife and our 20 great years of magic.

"Using Magic to Build Your Business is No Illusion, It's sound marketing principles and crowd pleasing psychology!"

-Yort Nagillim

Table of Contents

About the Author xi

Introduction 1

Chapter 1: Trade Show is Two Words. 5

Chapter 2: Ten Reasons You Need to Exhibit 11

Chapter 3: Choosing an Exhibiting Strategy 23
Setting Goals 23
Picking the Best Show to Attend 26
Setting a Budget 29
Writing an Action Plan. 32

Chapter 4: Pre-Show Marketing and Advertising 35
The Importance of Marketing. 36
One-on-One Appointments. 41
Utilize All Lines of Communication 43
Outsource It 44

Chapter 5: How to Get Free Publicity 47
Getting Your Company's Name in the Paper 47
How to Write a Press Release 50
Sample Press Release 53
Handling the Press at the Trade Show. 54

Chapter 6: Trade Show Promotional Materials 59
Premiums. 59
Literature 63

Chapter 7: Truth About Branding, Exhibit Design, and Signage 67

   Branding. 68

   Exhibit Design 70

   Signage 71

Chapter 8: Trade Show Displays 75

   Two Scenarios 75

   Equal Opportunity 77

   Booth Size. 77

   Types of Exhibits 80

Chapter 9: Exhibit Design 85

   Do It Yourself. 86

   Use an Exhibit Designer's Services 90

   Six Tips for Effective Exhibit Design 94

   Questions to Ask Yourself 98

   Exhibits, Not Just for Trade Shows 99

Chapter 10: The Importance of Training Booth Staff 103

   Create a Training Manual 106

   Staff Incentives 107

   Involvement of Salespeople .108

   Booth Etiquette 110

   Uniforms 113

   Unwanted Visitors 114

   The Importance of Teamwork. 115

   Conclusion. 117

Chapter 11: Lead Management 121

   Lead Sheet Creation 121

Sample Lead Sheet 124

Lead Sheet Management 125

Lead Manager 127

Chapter 12: Effective Presentations and

       Hospitality Events 131

Presentations 131

Presentation Techniques – Beginning to End 135

Demonstrations. 140

Hospitality Events 144

Chapter 13: The Use of Magic .149

Trade SHOW Business. 150

The Oldest Profession in the World 153

Hire a Professional Magician 154

Magician's Dress Code. 156

Tips for Magic Success 156

Success Story 158

Chapter 14: Exhibiting Logistics 161

Choosing a Location. 162

Know the Show Rules 165

Exhibit Insurance 166

Exhibit Restrictions. 167

Shipping the Exhibit. 168

Labor at the Show. 170

Document your Exhibit 172

Checklist Everything 173

Post-Show Shipping 175

Display Management. 176

Chapter 15: After The Show Ends. 179

    Post-Show Surveys. 179

    Budget Comparison 181

    Managing Leads 183

    Evaluating Your Success 185

Chapter 16: A Trade Show Veteran's

        Cost-Cutting Strategies. 191

Chapter 17: Lease your Exhibit 201

    Why Leasing is Better Than Bank Financing 202

    What is a Lease? 203

    Tax Benefits of Leasing. 205

    Accounting Benefits of Leasing 206

    How Credit Decisions are Often Made 208

    Use a Broker's Services 209

    Why Lease? 210

Glossary. 212

    Terms and Industry Lingo You Should Know

Bonus Sections 227

About the Author

By: Marianne Waterstradt, esq.

Troy Milligan knows the trade show industry as an exhibitor, a marketing and sales expert, a performer and a design consultant. His first exposure to trade shows was in 1975 when he was hired to dazzle attendees through the art of magic. He was immediately entranced by the entire trade show culture and understood from the outset that trade shows can be lucrative for both exhibitors and attendees. He was specifically intrigued at the lengths to which companies would go to show off their wares. Of course, he recognized from the beginning that magic can enhance trade show marketing and, over the years, he has worked virtually every venue imaginable. His skill is weaving a marketing message into a magical presentation that leaves the audience gasping in amazement. His experience has taught him that a marketing message woven into a magical moment is effective in such diverse sales environments as trade shows, product launches, business training, grand openings and even television commercials. As a professional magician and entrepreneur, Troy Milligan has reaped amazing rewards and enjoyed learning the secrets of marketing in a wholly unique way. In describing his experience, he often repeats a phrase he learned while traveling with the circus, "It's a hard way to make an easy living." Ultimately, he has learned that magic opens doors usually locked by skepticism and the rush of a hustle and bustle world. A moment of magic can make even the most hardened attendee stop and take notice. There is no question that magic also engenders creativity in developing a marketing presentation that turns the usual show into an exciting results-driven event.

Troy's experience doesn't come from simply attending trade shows like many others who claim an expertise in this arena. Troy Milligan has traveled around the world several times, performing in venues as diverse as corporate events and circus side shows. He has enjoyed the privilege of entertaining tens of thousands of people through his art. It wasn't until many years after he poured his energy into performing for the sake of entertainment that he refocused his energy on the trade show industry. Over the past nine years, he has used his 30+ years of performing and marketing talents to magically build one of America's most successful trade show marketing companies, www.capitalcityexhibits.com. In fact, Tradeshow Supermarket has consecutively doubled its sales volume for several years running. Tradeshow Supermarket delivers an unusual blend of creativity; customer service and competitive pricing that makes it stand far apart from the typical trade show distributor. From conceptual booth design to a complete marketing package with custom marketing presentations, Tradeshow Supermarket provides all the tools you'll need to make your next trade show your best ever! This is because

Capital City Exhibits, unlike its competitors, understands how to captivate attendees at the SHOW in a trade show.

Introduction

Being in a trade show shouldn't cost—it should pay! Whether you are on the cusp of exhibiting in your first trade show or you are a seasoned trade show veteran, the exhibiting tricks and secrets in this powerful book are sure to make your event wildly successful. In order to seriously prosper in the trade show environment, it is imperative that you hone in on the secrets of trade show marketing. Just imagine your marketing team having an aisle filled with prospective clients focused in on your live marketing presentation as your message is repeatedly delivered. In this book, you will learn tips and tricks that can instantly put more leads in reach of your marketing team, more sales on your books, and more return on your trade show investment than you ever imagined possible. You'll see how to lower your exhibiting cost and motivate your marketing team with results-driven management that is fun and profitable. <u>Milligan's Grab The Spotlight Checklist</u> alone will help you gain a surprising advantage over your competition. With the planning and media control explained in this book, you will propel your business onto the fast track of success. You'll be able to cut through the exhibiting guesswork with <u>Milligan's Trade Show Resource</u>

<u>Directory</u>, exclusively for trade show and convention professionals.

Every industry has a trade show. Whether you are a seller of pet products or a clothing designer, your industry has a trade show where the aisles teem with prospective clients interested in your widgets and eagerly searching for someone to ease their work challenges. To paraphrase an age-old maxim, it's like shooting fish in a barrel! I am convinced that, if your company cannot make a profitable showing in your industry's trade show, you likely should consider closing up shop. While that is a very strong comment, I believe it bears itself out 98% of the time. Most trade shows, even with their highly competitive nature, can be an easy and profitable opportunity for even the novice. Trade Shows don't have to be hard, and, in the words of the famous songwriter and actor Kris Kristofferson, "Even the worst I've had was good."

In this book, I'll provide a thorough overview of the steps you need to take to have an outrageously powerful trade show experience. From goal setting to designing an effective exhibit, and from pre-show marketing to properly managing leads, the subsequent chapters of this book walk you through a trade show plan that, if followed, will ensure your company's success as an exhibitor. It all starts with the realization that *trade show* is two words.

"The starting point of all achievement is desire. Keep this constantly in mind. Weak desires bring weak results."

Napoleon Hill, Author

Chapter 1 – Trade Show is Two Words

While this concept may seem quite simple, it is rarely even considered by potential trade show exhibitors. The trade, together with the show, creates a synergy that, when properly implemented, can explode into success. I believe the most overlooked part of the equation is the **SHOW.** Generally, companies are highly skilled and knowledgeable in their **TRADE,** possessing all the technical answers to a potential client's most obscure questions. But, when it comes to the **SHOW,** most fall quite flat. Trade shows are unique events where companies come together to exhibit their **TRADE** in front of a specific group of attendees that are there for the express purpose of seeking out your particular product or service. These events provide fantastic opportunities for sellers to showcase all their products and services. If you know the show biz secrets to performing in the **SHOW,** it won't matter that competitors are all exhibiting alongside one another in a dizzying array. It won't matter that they are all vying for the same customers. YOU and your company can make a splash that won't soon be forgotten. The big question is just how do you make that lasting impression as an exhibitor such that you can count your trade **SHOW** experience as one that will be beneficial to your company? How do you adequately prepare for the **SHOW** portion of the trade show? This book answers all those questions and more. You'll effectively see how to break down the long process of **SHOW** preparation into smaller steps that can be easily accomplished and result in more **TRADE** for your business.

As explained above, Trade Show is two words and both of these words get you nothing without marketing, Trade Show Marketing. When executed properly, Trade Show Marketing is a great way to see your company jump to the next level in terms of profitability. I am not talking about simply showing up at a trade show and standing in your booth. In today's competitive environment, this is no longer enough. Among the valuable tools presented in this book, you will learn how to create a live marketing presentation that can be delivered to your customers and prospects in a fun, exciting way. You will learn the small things that make the big difference, and you'll earn the rewards of exhibiting success.

If your company has made the decision to exhibit at an upcoming trade show and has put you in charge running the event, you might be anxious about how to make it worth the company's time and effort. Immediately, the flood of questions begins. What show will give your company the most bang for your trade show buck? What kind of booth will grab the attendees' attention? What should the booth staff say to make that all-important first impression? Rest at ease. This book will provide you with a comprehensive plan of action from start to finish. I understand the gravity of what is at stake, particularly in light of the fact that the trade show market consumes over $11 billion each year from companies just like yours. With those numbers on the line, each exhibiting experience should be orchestrated to offer the highest return. Wise exhibitors carefully use their investment capital to successfully reach their goals rather than wasting it on an ineffective method proven to be nothing more than a fleeting gimmick. I am certain that with a bit of creativity you can be the star of the show and walk away with much more than you invested.

Over the years, I have heard countless company heads express a common concern that trade shows are a waste of time and money. On the contrary, with proper planning, that is virtually never the case. I strongly believe that the key to trade show success lies in implementation. Many company executives have unrealistic goals in mind and have never been properly trained regarding the numerous forms of unique marketing a trade show setting offers. Moreover, I have found that many companies don't know why they are exhibiting in the first place, and consequently don't accurately measure the success of their exhibiting experience. This lack of follow-up results in the natural tendency to fold one's hands and proclaim defeat. The source of this unending circle of dissatisfaction is simple: Renting booth space, buying a display, and showing up with a stack of brochures does not make an exhibitor successful. Without the hook that captures your qualified prospects, you are just another cookie in the cookie cutter row of exhibitors looking for the easy sale. Qualified prospects are not automatically drawn to your booth with checkbooks in hand. Just like any other business venture, trade show exhibiting is not easy, nor should it be treated like a nuisance to be quickly disposed of and readily forgotten. Just one event properly planned and executed will result in long-term benefits that will surely be reaped for months and years to come.

"Ninety-nine percent of failures
come from people who have the habit
of making excuses."

– George Washington Carver, Botanist

Chapter 2 – Ten Reasons
You Need to Exhibit

Like all good books, it is important to first understand what is the foundation upon which all the bricks will be laid. Unless we explore what it is that will be gained by exhibiting, learning how to successfully do so is all but lost. That said, it is equally important to discuss the critical decision of what show is right for your company. It goes without saying that the correct show to exhibit in can be critical in ensuring a successful exhibiting experience. This one decision could mean the difference between leaving the show with those ever-valuable leads and leaving the show empty handed. That's part of the true beauty of exhibiting at the right show. Even if you aren't an expert at implementing the techniques in this book, you can still walk away with success.

On another note, you might be in a position of justifying your trade show investment to other members of your organization. Or, you might just want to understand exactly why it would be beneficial for your company to exhibit at an upcoming trade show. By now, you understand that just buying booth space and showing up simply isn't enough. To make it worth the time and money, companies must invest effort into planning and strategy for the show. This, while seemingly straight forward, is not an easy task. It requires superb organizational skills and the support of company management. But, before we discuss the planning stages, let's explore why you would want to exhibit your company's products or services at a trade show in the first place. The following are the top ten reasons that a company may choose to exhibit at a trade show:

1.   **Lower Sales Cost** – A trade show is certainly an investment and, like all advertising, comes with no guarantees. But, after you add up such costs as booth space, exhibit display, marketing, and travel, you will find that the price tag is often a far better investment as compared to other forms of advertising. This is the principle annunciated at the beginning of this book. Being in a trade show should pay not cost! Unlike traditional shotgun advertising that randomly hits almost everything whether interested in your offer or not, a trade show provides the unique opportunity to target specific leads and qualify prospects within a very short time frame. Indeed, as compared to

sending your sales team out into the field, you will quickly find that target marketing prospects in the confines of a tradeshow is markedly less expensive both in time and dollars. Prospects are there expressly to learn about your particular product or service, your only job is to qualify them and present your information to them in an exciting yet concise format. While the national average cost of closing a sale following a trade show is $218.00, the average cost of tracking a lead and closing a sale out in the field is over three times higher at $657.00! You can see how, if executed properly, your sales strategy at a trade show will more than make up for the time and money invested in exhibiting.

2. **Portable Marketing** – By exhibiting at a trade show, a company gets to turn itself into a portable unit for the duration of the show. Your company's image is projected directly to the show attendees, who were driven to the show by their interest in the very type of product or service you have to offer. Since the attendees at trade shows are often sincerely interested in what exhibitors have to show them, exhibitors have the rare opportunity to present themselves to many qualified prospects within a short period of time. Attendees are free to interact with you personally, ask questions, and test out your products in a live setting. In large part, the trade show settings is as if these prospective clients gathered together and stormed your office looking for your product or service. Imagine how excited your sales team would be if busloads of pro-

spective clients filed through your office asking to learn about your product or service. With a trade show, this unique opportunity becomes reality. Similarly, the company should look at exhibiting as a way to take your sales office out to the crowds and give them all the tools they need to capture those sales.

3. **Marketing to the Decision-Makers** – Partly due to the recent political and security issues facing the world, fewer attendees are coming to trade shows than they did before 911. While at first you may think that this is a reason not to invest time and effort into exhibiting, it is actually a compelling reason to do precisely the opposite. Since fewer company representatives are taking the time to travel to trade shows, of those that do attend, a greater percentage are genuinely interested in keeping up with the latest trends in the industry. Not only that, those attendees are often the ones with real buying power. In fact, about three quarters of show attendees are people who hold managerial positions within their firms. These are people that have often times traveled a great distance, sometimes hundreds of miles, to see how they can meet a current need or desire within their company. If you are fortunate enough to be a company that markets to the public at large, you can be sure that those people willing to travel to a trade show are likewise there with a goal in mind and ready to realize that goal. These decision-makers, whether corporate or individual, usually come to the shows ready to make purchasing decisions on the spot or shortly afterwards. Even

though most of us are experienced and competent sales-people, we have all been after that one seemingly promising prospect with numerous phone calls and visits, only to discover that we have been speaking with the wrong person in the organization from the very outset. A trade show setting all but eliminates this problem since there is usually such a high concentration of decision-makers in attendance. It is an excellent opportunity for a salesperson to be able to pitch their product directly to the people in charge without wasting time.

4. **Launching Pad for New Products** – Trade shows provide a great opportunity for a company to launch its new products or services into the marketplace. Along with showing your established line of products, you have the opportunity to showcase your new and newly improved items directly to the buying masses. The pre-show and at-the-show marketing plan that you implement can enable your company to cost-effectively reach thousands of potential buyers who are interested in seeing your new products or services in action. Since the buyers come to you, trade show demonstrations are generally less expensive but pack a hearty punch. A trade show also offers a venue for cost effective, on the spot, market research. In addition, you can measure the effectiveness of your presentation style and content by conducting short surveys either at the show or immediately following it. The results of which are a better understanding of your clients and their needs.

5. **Competition Research** – Let's face it, at most trade shows exhibitors find themselves going head to head with their competitors for the very same prospects. This is even more so in a trade show setting where the orientation of the show is aimed at one particular industry. In fact, you might find yourself only a few booths away from your strongest competitor. If that scares you away, it shouldn't. It should just give you more reasons to exhibit. In the first place, you will be given the rare opportunity to research your competition throughout the duration of the show. For example, you can check out what your competition is doing by occasionally taking a little stroll past their booth. By doing this, you can see what image they are projecting to the attendees, what kind of literature are they handing out, whether they have a crowd, how their sales people are drawing attendees to their booth. There are myriad pieces of information to be garnered in this simple way. You should also be sure to ask yourself if they have a way of doing things that you particularly like or dislike and which of their practices could you implement for your own company's benefit. As we all know, it is never wise to badmouth your competition, but much can be learned by listening to the comments your prospects make about the competition at the show. It is no secret that many attendees come to trade shows to comparison shop giving you a great opportunity to outshine the rest.

6. **Company Image** – Naturally, not every company is as well known, liked and respected, as its owners would

like it to be. Trade shows provide an excellent opportunity for a company to polish that image and stand out from the crowd. By preparing for the show correctly, you can reinforce your company's good image and even improve the perception your company now enjoys. Often times at a trade show, the people walking the aisles will be new potential prospects who have yet to be exposed to your company. With all these fresh eyes and ears perked to hear your message, the opportunity is ripe to present your products and services in a unique and compelling way. Even though you may find it difficult to measure the effectiveness of this aspect of exhibiting, the effort put into building and polishing your presentation will not escape the attention of show attendees. Not only do you expose yourself to thousands of attendees and qualified prospects, but also present are members of the media. They have the power to use the written word to your advantage, and conversely, to your disadvantage. It is crucial to handle the media to enhance the perception of your company. It is often said you only get one chance to make a great first impression. That maxim bears itself out more so in the trade show setting than anywhere. Attendees have little time to make a decision about your company, make it easy for them to make the right decision with a striking presentation and a courteous approach. That said, it is equally important make a great last impression which can be even more powerful.

7. **New Distribution Channels** – By exhibiting at a trade show, a company can open itself up to a whole new world of opportunities. Exhibiting allows you to meet and establish relationships with various new partners. A good trade show will attract numerous companies from the same industry, thus giving them the opportunity to interact with each other and form new relationships. Since personal contact is the norm at a trade show, you can find new qualified representatives who are ready to go out and sell your product. You can also meet new vendors who may be willing and able to complement your product offering. Trade shows are also a great way to reconnect with some of your current sales representatives and vendors by allowing them to share space in your booth. This cuts exhibiting costs for all parties involved and is a great way to promote more active selling of your products and services.

8. **Time-Tested Method** – Through economic booms and recessions, and even through the advent of the Internet and other new forms of communication, trade shows have withstood the test of time in virtually every industry and every geographic area of our country. Although there are those who believe that trade shows are an unnecessary expense, the fact is, if your company plays its cards right, you can recover your exhibiting expenses many times over. Your company can benefit from exhibiting just like numerous companies have over the years. If you happen to find out that some of your competition is not going

to exhibit this year, I suggest you consider that an even stronger reason for you to exhibit. Your company will gain valuable exposure to current and future customers by doing so.

9.   **The Ultimate Marketing Experience** – Exhibiting at a trade show is the ultimate marketing experience; it incorporates public relations, sales promotion, advertising, and the opportunity to make personal contacts and one-on-one sales. No other business activity allows a company to concentrate all of its marketing efforts towards one goal like a trade show does. The extent and frequency of one-on-one marketing and communication that happens at trade shows cannot be duplicated out in the field. In fact, it would take your salespeople months in the field to make the same number of quality contacts that can be made in a few hours within the confines of a trade show. Even such a vital thing as product demonstration can be done so much more efficiently if it's done at a trade show where customers come to you. Therefore, the investment you make into your various marketing channels in preparation for the show will be well worth it in the long run.

10. **Personal Contact** – As human beings, we have been conditioned from childhood to learn in a visual and interactive fashion. A trade show setting accommodates this need all of us have for personal contact. In these modern times, almost any product or service can be purchased over the telephone or over the Internet. Despite this,

experience has shown that people still choose to travel hundreds of miles to attend trade shows where they have the chance to personally interact with the sellers. People want to see welcoming faces and great products which, in turn, smoothes the buying pathway. By virtue of a trade show setting allowing for adequate personal interaction, there is usually no additional personal visit required to the prospect's location before they become your company's client. This is why it is more crucial than ever to make your presence known at a trade show by way of pre-show marketing efforts, and to train your staff properly. You want your prospects to come to you eager to learn about what you have to offer them. A trade show is the perfect environment to make the most of the rare personal interaction with your prospects.

In addition to these ten reasons for exhibiting at trade shows, there may be other reasons that your company may choose to exhibit. Most of the time, when companies prioritize their exhibiting goals, they do so by the degree to which each goal can reduce their cost of sales. Not all of the above ten reasons for exhibiting may appeal to you. However, based on your industry and your company's culture, you may or may not want to utilize the benefits of all ten of the above reasons. Find what works for you. Brainstorm with your team to get to the bottom of what's really important to your organization. Then, get down to the business of deciding how to create a positive show experience for your company.

"A great flame follows a little spark."

– Dante Alighieri, Poet

Chapter 3 – Choosing an Exhibiting Strategy

SETTING GOALS

Why Should You Exhibit?

One of the first questions that should be addressed is why your company would want to exhibit at a trade show. More importantly, what factors would make the show a success in your eyes and the eyes of management? Consider the following four-trade show objectives that will help guide your decision:

1. Increasing sales and reinforcing market share

2. Getting new customers and keeping current customer base

3.   Introducing new products or services

4.   Establishing your company's image and positioning your place in the market

As you can see, these objectives tie in closely with the reasons that companies have for exhibiting, which were discussed in the previous chapter. You may think, your business is unlike any other; everyone thinks that way but business is business. Whether you are a company that sells computer technology or one that sells paperclips, your business can exponentially grow from implementing the foregoing objectives. In fact, these objectives may and should be tailored to suit your specific situation. To be sure, the way companies differ is far less than the ways that they are alike. No matter what industry you are in, or how big or small your company is, it is crucial to make sure that these objectives are being met by your presence at the right trade show.

Pinpoint Your Target.

Most professionals, like yourself, have heard it said time and again that goal setting works. Setting a goal before attending a trade show is no different in this regard. In my experience, I find that the biggest reason most companies fail when they exhibit at trade shows is that they never make the concrete step of setting goals before attending the show. Management finds out there's a show coming up, hears that some of their competitors may be exhibiting, so they decide to rent booth space, buy a display, and show up brochures in hand. This lessez faire attitude of letting the chips fall as they may contributes heavily to the lack of success experienced by most exhibitors. Even assuming the booth staff understands the purpose of attending the show, they have no written or even verbalized goals to guide their performance. If your goals are not in writing, then they're not goals. Rather, they are mere illusion taking the form of dreams and wishes. There's no way to track unwritten goals, to continuously make sure they're being met, and to evaluate them following the show. I compare this to trying to aim and hit a bullseye with a dagger while blindfolded. First, you're not sure how large or small the target is, you haven't an idea of where it is and you don't know how far you are from it. Absent being a professional knife thrower, such as myself, you haven't much of a chance. So it is absolutely crucial to sit down with your team and brainstorm specific, quantifiable goals for exhibiting at a trade show before committing your company's time and money.

Write it Down.

Your management team has to determine exactly why it is that your company should exhibit. You might be interested in simply polishing your image to those potential clients that might not know your company as well as you would like. On the other hand, you might be looking for sales, sales, sales. Or, your goal could be generating and collecting leads to be pursued at a later time. Any of the foregoing may be on your mind or perhaps, like most exhibitors, it is a combination of those together with other endeavors your company is seeking. You need to ask yourself what will make exhibiting at a show successful for your company. Again, is it closing sales, promotion, or another goal? What is most important is to make these goals as specific and detailed as possible. Put them down in writing and follow through on them. If the goals are not written down and communicated clearly to your trade show team, you might as well be wishing for a pot of gold or buying a handful of lottery tickets. Your show goals have to be specific, measurable, and relevant to your organization. It is only with this type of careful planning and strict execution that you can assure the success your company is seeking.

PICKING THE BEST SHOW TO ATTEND

Once you have put your exhibiting goals in writing and have confirmed with your team what and how those goals are to be achieved, it is time to start choosing which show will best serve your needs. In fact, within any one industry there can literally be dozens of shows in which your company can make a showing. They vary in size, location, objectives, and the type of exhibitors and attendees they attract. As we have discussed, in light of the substantial investment that will accompany exhibiting at any show you choose, you should undertake a thorough analysis before committing your resources. Below are some guidelines to consider in making this important decision.

Choose a Show Based on Your Goals.

When it comes to choosing the best trade show for your company, much depends on what you have determined are your primary exhibiting goals. If you have written those goals at this point, take them out and review what is important to your company. If you haven't yet written down what it is you are trying to accomplish with your exhibiting experience, you should take the time to do so now. Now that you have that ever important road map to your destination, you can start to narrow your choices of where to showcase your company. If you are looking at creating name and brand recognition within your industry, you will probably want to find a show that is more heavily attended by those in your industry rather than by lay people. For example, in the trade show industry we have two major events each year. The EXHIBITOR show and TS2, these shows are almost exclusively attended by exhibit retailers and distributors within the industry. This is in stark contrast to a show that is attended by people who are coming to a show to purchase a particular product or service. In order to better gauge what type of shows are offered in your trade, I recommend you obtain a prospectus from each show that you are considering, and carefully look over the objectives that each show management team is striving to achieve. Are the objectives of the management team in line with your company's exhibiting objectives? If so, this is likely the right show for you.

Where is Your Audience?

Along the same line of thought, you should be careful to pinpoint your company's target audience and make sure that group will be in full force at the show you select. The obvious purpose for taking this issue into consideration is that without your target audience attending the show, you won't have the fertile ground to sew your marketing seeds. Again, you don't want to waste your company's trade show dollar by making a presence at a show where the attendees have no interest or need in your product or service. If your company sells accounting software designed for the boating industry, you shouldn't exhibit at an inkjet printer's convention and expect great results. I suggest that you contact the organizers of the shows that your are considering and ask questions about the prospective attendees. They should be happy to provide you with a profile of their attendees from past years. By evaluating this information, you can be sure to locate a show whose attendees profile closely aligns with your current or desired market.

Where is Your Competition?

A parallel issue to be considered is your competition. While so many companies shy away from this daring exercise, I suggest that the more competitors you anticipate being at a particular show, the better a show it is for your company to attend. While not obvious at first blush, the reason for my position is really quite simple. By positioning yourself among your competitors, you have the rare chance to compete side by side rather than at arm's length. You can immediately dispel any notions that you haven't the same quality product or service your competitors proclaim to have. Further, you can easily outshine those that haven't undertaken the concrete pre-show preparations you have. In addition, you have the unprecedented opportunity to scrutinize their sales means and methods, giving you the ability to generate a strategy to outsmart them in the marketplace of ideas now and in the future. Finally, by physically positioning your booth within close proximity to an industry leader, you can attract their prospects as they parade along the trade show floor right past your booth. As an aside, if your competitors foolishly choose not to attend this year's event, you can use that shortcoming to your advantage. You are sure to benefit by having a presence at the show, and may even attract some of your competition's prospective or existing customers to your booth.

Go as an Attendee.

If your company is brand new to the trade show arena, it is wise to first attend a trade show as an attendee. Choose a show that you are considering, and walk the floor as an observer. Walk the aisles, talk with different exhibitors, and see various displays. Take thorough notes on what appeals to you and what doesn't, the layout, the number of attendees, and the companies exhibiting. Before investing time and money in exhibiting, you will greatly benefit from seeing the show from the aisle rather than from the booth.

SETTING A BUDGET

Once your exhibiting goals are set and you have selected the perfect show, it is now time to set your exhibiting budget. The most important thing to remember is to set a budget that is in line with your exhibiting goals. Your budget should reasonably accommodate the purchase of all tools and the expense of time necessary to reach your goals. Since your company has probably set aside a limited amount of funds for trade shows, it is obviously paramount to stay within these parameters while making each trade show dollar count. If your company has exhibited in the past, you can review those expenses and get a sense of how much you will need. Keep in mind that there are many ways of cutting costs and getting the most for your money when exhibiting. Numerous cost-cutting strategies will be discussed in subsequent chapters. For now, review the following six basic categories of expenses that you are sure to encounter when allocating parts of your budget:

1. Exhibit costs – Your exhibit will certainly last through a number of shows. Accordingly, it is best to make sure that you don't choose your exhibit based on price alone. Cheaper exhibits, while less costly at the outset, often require more repairs, resulting in a greater outlay over time. Of course, if you don't plan to repeatedly exhibit, you can consider renting a display for one or two shows.

2. Booth Space – When renting booth space at a show, it is imperative that you sit down and seriously assess how much space you will need to achieve your exhibiting goals. By following some simple recommendations, which you will find in subsequent chapters, you can ensure that you don't overspend, or, for that matter, underspend, in this category.

3. Pre-show marketing –You must be careful to allocate the proper percentage of your budget for pre-show marketing. Too often companies miss this important step re-

sulting in a less-than-successful exhibiting experience. Proper pre-show marketing strategies highly increase the likelihood that you will attract desired attendees to your booth.

4. <u>Show staffing and training</u> – Too few booth staff or too many can have the same negative impact. During the high traffic times, your booth should be fully manned for maximum effectiveness. Similarly, too many people in a slower traffic time may leave attendees intimidated to approach a booth teeming with hungry sales staff. The balance, while seemingly difficult to find, is calculable as described in more detail below. Although training your salespeople for the show can be expensive and time-consuming, the investment is more than worth the expense.

5. <u>Transportation of staff and exhibit</u> –Both materials and people will have to be transported to the show. Because the best show for your goals may entail driving or flying long distances, you should consider the costs associated therewith. Those costs include storage of display equipment, hotel, and entertainment. Make sure the arrangements are settled as far in advance as possible.

6. <u>Show services</u> – There are many options when it comes to selecting your sources for labor, booth setup, and other services. As far as the show management allows, be sure to shop around for the best rates and terms.

WRITING AN ACTION PLAN

As successful businessmen and businesswomen, we don't start a big project without first writing down a detailed plan of action. This is aside from the goal writing exercise described above. Your action plan should include every detail and should leave nothing to chance. All team members are to be aware of exactly what events are to take place and when each planned event is to happen. Your action plan should include all events from the time you decide to exhibit to the time your last lead has received a follow-up contact. Consider the following questions and expand them to establish a customized, thorough plan of action for your company's exhibiting endeavor:

- Who will select and rent booth space?

- When will the display be ordered?

- When will show services be ordered?

- How will staff and equipment arrive at the show?

- Who is responsible for what before, during, and after the show?

- What is expected of every staff member?

- Who is responsible for setup and dismantling the display?

By creating a thorough list and holding team members accountable for the completion of all items, you will ensure that things get done the right way, the first time.

**"I find that the harder I work,
the more luck I seem to have."**

– Thomas Jefferson, US President

Chapter 4 – Pre-Show Marketing and Advertising

First off, let me congratulate you. If you've come this far in the book, chances are that your company has decided to exhibit at an upcoming trade show. Because you clearly see the benefits of exhibiting and you have already set your exhibiting goals, you surely want to understand precisely how to make your company's exhibiting experience as successful as possible.

As your company prepares to exhibit at a trade show, you will undoubtedly have extensive contact with an exhibit manufacturer who will design and put together a professional display for you. Most display companies can also perform numerous additional tasks for you based on your needs and your budget. Aside from the design and purchase of the display unit itself, your exhibit company can take care of the logistics of delivering the display to the show venue, making hotel reservations for you, planning your needs for contracted labor at the show, and other services. What exhibit companies generally don't assist with, however, is your pre-show marketing plan. It has been my experience that most 'one-stop-shops' lack the knowledge and resources to set up a definitive marketing plan for your company. Since this element of your exhibiting strategy is so essential in attracting a crowd, hitting your target market, and getting the leads you want, you should be sure to take advantage of my **FREE "*Trade Show Marketing Consultation*"** (see certificate located in the bonus section at the back of this book).

THE IMPORTANCE OF MARKETING

On average across industries, less than 23 percent of exhibitors do any kind of pre-show promotion. Most companies buy a display, rent booth space, and show up with plenty of brochures. Their sales representatives stand in shifts in their booth and talk to anybody that randomly ambles by. They often give away a "personalized" souvenir such as a stuffed bear or pens inscribed with the company logo, but they often fail even to request this prospective client's business card. What is unfortunate is that these seemingly aggressive contacts are actually wasting their time and their company's money. Although it may seem an effective way to make contact with the sea of prospects floating past, it is certainly no way to exhibit successfully at a trade show. In fact, most attendees come to a trade show already knowing which companies' booths they want to visit. By failing to make that ever important pre-show contact and getting on that short list of interesting companies, you are missing out on a world of opportunity. In an ideal world, you want to be the one hot company that most attendees come to see. In reality, however, you need to invest in some pre-show marketing in order to get as many attendees to come see you as possible.

Customers

An often-overlooked group when planning your pre-show marketing campaign is your company's current customers. Your current customer base is very important and a rich source of continuing revenue. As such, they should be a top priority when sending out your pre-show marketing message. Wise business people keep in regular contact with former customers and your upcoming show gives you a solid purpose to contact them again further reinforcing your relationship with them. A face-to-face encounter may be just the thing to spur new ways in which you can help them with your product or service.

You can mail them a postcard, a personalized letter, or even make a personal phone call letting them know when and where your company will be exhibiting. I suggest a personalized, typed letter to communicate with your current customers, but only you can determine the most appropriate way to effectively reach your customer base. You should direct their attention to the benefits they will receive by visiting your exhibit. Do you have a new product that you are sure they will be interested in? Have you improved a process that will be beneficial to their operations? Make sure to communicate this clearly in your pre-show marketing campaign to clarify why it is to their benefit to attend the show and visit your booth. Of course it is worthy of repetition that you should make certain their visit is greeted with care and their continued patronage recognized.

And, for those with that extra zeal, you can even notify your clients of an airfare sale or a group discount at a hotel that may be of interest or assistance to them. This satisfies the twin aims of providing them with valuable information that could encourage their attendance at the show and providing you an additional point of contact.

Prospects

The next group you should heavily market in your preshow campaign is your company's current prospects and leads. Your sales team surely has lists of companies that they have recently called on. Certainly you are aware of companies that have bought from your partners or representatives in the past. Perhaps you can sway them to buy from your company in the future. Combine these lists, and you will have a comprehensive database of hot prospects to market.

Again, there are myriad methods to reach this group. I suggest mailing an oversized postcard. The postcard is relatively inexpensive to develop, cheap to mail, and, if designed properly, can give your prospects all of the necessary information about your upcoming exhibit. A postcard has the advantage that it is more likely to be read by the addressee because it doesn't require the reader to open an envelope. The oversized postcard has the added advantage that it can grab even the most impenetrable mail screener and ultimately arrive on the desk of a qualified prospect. To help you get started with postcard marketing, I've arranged a special deal to get you wholesale pricing on full color postcards. See the bonus section in the back of this book.

Just as with your current clients, make sure that your communication expressly states the advantage of attending the show and seeking out your booth. Keep in mind that in all of your marketing pieces you must be sure to follow through on your promises. For example, if your marketing piece requests them to bring the postcard in exchange for a special gift, be certain to have something of value especially geared toward those clients or prospects. If your promise is to offer a special pricing structure to those that meet certain criteria, make sure your sales team is well aware of the promotion and prepared to make the sale on the promised terms. Disappointing those that made the extra effort to seek you out will do much more to injure your reputation than not having made any promises at all. In fact, your goal should be to exceed the expectations of those seeking out the product or service you provide. Only in this way can you increase the likelihood that you will be remembered when the time to exercise the final purchasing decision comes to fruition.

Potentials

When it comes to this third target group and pre-show marketing, the defining lines grow a little dim. This group consists of companies you suspect would be good prospects for your product or service but you haven't solidified your belief. I call these the "potentials." You can begin to determine who a good potential prospect will be for your company by consulting with your staff. Your marketing and sales managers, as well as your product managers, should be able to tell you whom they would consider a good prospect.

Once you know the profile of the kind of person or company you should be targeting, you should obtain specialized lists from list management companies. You can purchase mailing lists based on industry, geographic location, company size, or other relevant parameters. These lists assist in the difficult task of narrowing down the prospect pool to only those that are most promising. Similarly, you can obtain lists from the publishers of trade journals in your industry or from your professional association. Another avenue of approach is to obtain a list from the trade show management team that can further refine your potentials.

Once you have compiled an extensive list of potentials to market, you can choose your marketing scheme. You can send a fax or email to those with whom you have a current business relationship, you can send the same oversized postcard, or you can make a personal telephone contact. The postcard mailing can include an incentive for those that make their way to your booth such as an entry into a drawing or a free gift.

Another valuable marketing tool is to invite people to visit your website where they can enter your contest. You can then announce the winner during or at the conclusion of a show presentation. In any event, you should be sure to emphasize what is to be won. The prize must be something that will be of value to your potentials and will be sufficient to entice them to visit your booth.

A great way to acknowledge all of those that took the time to register for your contest is to award an additional gift as a second place prize. Providing a second place prize offers you the opportunity to contact all those that entered the drawing but did not win. The prize can be as simple as a discount on orders placed within the subsequent two months or a special bonus with purchase. But, again, be sure this second place prize has some value in the eyes of your potential customers.

For a special resource directory loaded with companies offering specialty products that work well within the trade show arena, please see the bonus section under "Free Resource Guide" at the conclusion of this book. The resource directory will save you valuable time and put you on the right track to finding that perfect incentive.

ONE-ON-ONE APPOINTMENTS

Your marketing pieces should be on their way to your target groups at least one month prior to the show date. This lead time will permit your clients, prospects and potentials sufficient time to make arrangements to attend the show should they so choose. Similarly, the lead time gives you the time to follow up on your mailings whether by telephone, email or another means of communication.

Another crucial aspect of your pre-show marketing is to seek a one-on-one show appointment with your target groups. You should include a request for such a meeting in your marketing pieces. In the event you have a current business relationship with a target, you can go as far as presetting the meeting with a date and time. This gives you a jump on your competition and many of your targets will adhere to the schedule and appreciate your aggressive approach. This method, however, should be reserved only for those clients with whom you have a close working relationship. Taking this approach with all your targets will certainly put some of them off. Once you send out the pre-show marketing pieces, you should place that ever important follow up call. During this call, you can explain to your target the content of your meeting and offer the opportunity to reschedule if the allotted time is inconvenient. Even though you may feel awkward making such proposals at first, you will find that interested prospects will be flattered at the personal invitation. There is no reason that, with careful planning, you can't have a number of pre-set appointments even before the show starts.

If your company decides to host a hospitality function in the nearby hotel or in another setting during the show, your pre-show marketing pieces should invite your customers and prospects to attend your function. You can invite your prospects to your booth to pick up an invitation. This provides yet another enticement to visit your booth.

UTILIZE ALL LINES OF COMMUNICATION

During those valuable pre-show months, all your company's regular correspondence, specifically mail and email, should include a reference to your upcoming show. Advertising your upcoming exhibit on invoices, email, voicemail messages and other forms of communication is also cost effective.

If your company regularly sends newsletters, you should be sure to include a feature article highlighting your decision to exhibit. Likewise, if you have a website, you should design a page specifically geared toward advertising the upcoming show. Any mailings should also include a reference to your company's website where you can provide your prospects with more in depth information regarding the products and services you intend to highlight at the show. Using your existing website to enhance your pre-show marketing efforts is not only effective, it is virtually cost free.

It bears repeating that all of your pre-show marketing material should explain how the customer will benefit by coming to see your exhibit, and should encourage your target group to set up a one-on-one appointment with you.

As an additional method of pre-show advertising, you may consider placing an advertisement in a trade publication or in the show directory. This will attract attention from a segment of the market that you might otherwise have missed. Again, the advertisement should direct the reader to your company's website, which will give them more details on your upcoming exhibit.

The main goal of all your pre-show marketing efforts

should be consistency and simplicity. Your marketing message should be clear and easy to understand, and it should support your show objectives.

OUTSOURCE IT

If the task of conducting a full-fledged pre-show marketing campaign seems overwhelming to you, I assure you that you are not alone. Successful implementation of such a campaign does require a lot of organization, teamwork, and planning. Every member of the trade show planning team should have an adequate amount of responsibility for their portion of the work, and should be held accountable for completing it in a timely manner.

However, if your team decides that this is too much to take on in addition to your daily workload, don't despair. You can outsource all of your pre-show marketing to companies that specialize in precisely this type of advertising campaign. For a fee, they will take over the task of mailing, calling, faxing, and setting up appointments for you. You have to decide if this expense can fit into your exhibiting budget. Ultimately, your job is to assure that the pre-marketing is done whether you undertake the task yourself or outsource the task. Taking this one important step will easily double your tradeshow dollar and generate benefits for months and years to come.

"Every idea you present must be something you could get across easily at a cocktail party with strangers."

– *Jack Welch – GE Chief Executive*

Chapter 5 – How to Get Free Publicity

GETTING YOUR COMPANY'S NAME IN THE PAPER

How many times have you opened the newspaper to the business section and been captured by a particularly impressive advertisement? We have all had the experience of seeing a colorful discussion of the latest and greatest new product from Procter & Gamble, GM, or Sony. While reading, we immediately imagine the droves of new customers reading the same article and flocking to the store, checkbook in hand. We think with envy, "These companies must hold the secret to getting their name in the paper." They do and now you will too. As promised, read on to learn the secret of getting your name as prominently highlighted as any of the big companies for a fraction of the cost you might expect.

The first step to getting this valuable yet inexpensive publicity is to write a powerful press release and submit it to the right sources. This seemingly insignificant step serves the purpose of getting your information in front of someone who can, and often will, highlight your company in a significant medium at no cost to you. Let me explain. As you know, a typical full page advertisement in a major newspaper would likely run anywhere from 5,000 to 15,000 dollars for a single day's run. If you are able to capture the attention of the newspaper editor with a powerful press release, you could find your company's news story taking the very place of that advertisement you would have paid rather handsomely for. As is readily apparent, creating an effective press release can save you hundreds, if not thousands, of dollars. In addition, this cost cutting strategy will permit you to allocate money otherwise earmarked for advertising to other valuable areas.

As you can see, having a press story printed about your company is very much like getting free advertising except that, in many ways, it's even better. You see, since you are providing all of the facts on your company and your upcoming exhibit, information that you couldn't fit into an advertisement will nonetheless be printed right there in full living color. In addition, print media is a more effective medium than radio or television because it is almost always viewed as more credible. By writing an effective press release, you will gain exposure in the public's eye, build awareness of your company, and introduce new products to the public, all without spending a mint.

Paul Hartunian, in his seminar "How To Get A Million Dollars in Free Publicity," talks about how to write an effective press release that will get noticed by reporters and, ultimately, published. And he has good reason to explain this principle and has seen it borne out time and again. In fact, he is the man that sold the Brooklyn Bridge and made a fortune doing it. Paul got international press coverage almost overnight and developed a step-by-step formula that anyone can follow. His experience shows that the best way to get the word out about a company is to submit a well written press release to various local and national newspapers and radios. Since reporters are always looking for a newsworthy story to write, you will find that the response to your submitted press release is largely positive. Even if you submit your story to dozens of newspapers around the country but find that only a handful are willing to publish it, count yourself a success. As noted above, the papers that do publish your story will give your company credibility and heighten the public's awareness of what you have to offer. That is the case whether it's just the local community paper that chooses to publish your story or the New York Times. You can then collect those newspaper clippings and incorporate them into your pre-show advertising campaign. When your prospects, clients and potentials see your company's name splashed across the front page of the business section, they will ascribe credibility and newsworthiness to your company.

HOW TO WRITE A PRESS RELEASE

The cornerstone to getting your story published in a newspaper is to write a gripping press release. By pouring over the many sources discussing this topic and adding my own proven techniques, I have been able to compile the following tricks and tips that will assist you in writing your own effective press release. Keep in mind that, while it is important to follow these steps somewhat closely, you will have to be flexible in order to adopt them to fit your organization's structure.

1. Write your press release on a plain 8 ½" by 11" sheet of white paper. Do not use your company letterhead, otherwise you will instantly show the reporter your lack of knowledge in the game of publicity. A press release written on company letterhead has very little chance of being read by a reporter.

2. Leave a one-inch margin around the text, and double space the text.

3. Start out with the phrase "For Immediate Release" in the upper left hand corner. To the right, print a contact name, address, and phone number. The contact name should be yours, or somebody else's in your organization that is completely aware of the story that is being sent to the press.

4. Keep your press release to one page. It should be short, simple, and to the point. The writing style should be at the reading level of a smart eighth grader; not too com-

plicated for the reporter or the general public to read. If you don't have great writing skills, ask somebody else to write the press release for you.

5. Your press release should always answer the five basic questions: who, what, why, when and where.

6. Make sure to time your press release correctly. If you are announcing your new product at the next trade show, make sure to send out the press release enough in advance so that it gets printed before the show.

7. It's best to fax your press release directly to the attention of the reporter who handles the local or national news. Follow up with a phone call to the reporter, and your story will most likely get published. Reporters are looking for good stories to print, and you are almost doing them a favor if you send a good story their way. If you don't want to spend the time faxing out your press release across the country, there are services such as the AP Newswire that will do this for you for a fee. Also, once your press release is published, there are fee-based services that will collect your newspaper clippings from all across the country for you.

8. Your press release should start out with a catchy headline that describes exactly what the news is. The first paragraph is the most important and should include the who, where, what, when and why of the story. The second paragraph should contain testimonials that show your cred-

ibility to the reporter and to the general public. The last paragraph should briefly give your contact information. By including your contact information in your piece, you are giving the readers a chance to contact you directly and bypass calling the reporter for the information.

9.   Your press release should end with three hash marks. This is like the "pound" symbol on a phone, and it signifies the end of the story.

On the following page is a sample press release that I have successfully used several times with minor changes from time to time. It incorporates all of the above points and is a simple example of how uncomplicated the press release writing process should be.

SAMPLE PRESS RELEASE

FOR IMMEDIATE RELEASE

For further information contact:
Troy Milligan – (916) 631-9900

Donations Available For Local Charities

Capital City Exhibits a Rancho Cordova based company that provides display systems and banner stands to companies worldwide is offering to donate quantities of its merchandise to local charitable and community-orientated organizations. This merchandise includes pop up display frames; banner stands, portable panel displays, and other trade show related accessories.

The organizations receiving items are free to sell them or use them to assist in promoting their cause in any way they see fit.

A spokesman for Tradeshow Supermarket has said that the company will donate up to $20,000 worth of merchandise to one or more local Sacramento area organizations.

"This merchandise will be freely given away to the organizations with no strings attached. The Sacramento community has been very good to us. This is simple an effective way for us to give back to the community."

If your organization is interested in receiving some of this merchandise, send a brief note, including a phone number, explaining the purpose of your organization to: Troy Milligan, 11345 Trade Center Drive, Suite 450, Rancho Cordova, CA 95742. No phone calls or drop ins, please.

###

HANDLING THE PRESS AT THE TRADE SHOW

While it may not seem obvious to those that don't frequently exhibit at a trade show, you should be aware that members of the press commonly attend and walk the aisles of trade shows. Their purpose for attending trade shows is to get the scoop on interesting new products and services that are soon to be launched into the marketplace. Press members are often affiliated with a trade show daily publication, the various journals of professional associations, or even newspapers and magazines. You should contrive a set plan in advance for how you will attract the press to your booth.

One quick way to ascertain who the press are is to pay attention to the attendee badge colors. Members of the press are generally distinguished by badge colors. For instance, exhibitors might be assigned blue badges, attendees might be assigned red badges but the press will likely sport an entirely different color such as yellow. With that in mind, you should instruct every member of your team to have a sharp eye out for members of the press meandering down the aisles. You should carefully assess which member of your team is particularly articulate and comfortable speaking and assign him or her the role of speaking to the press on your company's behalf. The moment one of your team spots the press badge; your spokesperson should make an express effort to engage the press member in conversation. The press should be offered your product presentation immediately, and they should be rewarded with a nice premium as a thank you for stopping by your booth.

Your conversation with members of the press should focus strictly on your company's marketing message, your products and services, and the benefits that they provide to your customers. It is also a wise idea to have a pre-assembled press kit readily on hand for easy distribution. The press kit should include information on new product releases, photos, and other company literature. If there is a separate press room at the trade show venue, you should make sure that it is stocked with copies of your press kit at the beginning of each day.

Avoid Embarrassment

Although the foregoing heading may seem readily apparent, a word of caution is warranted. Sometimes, members of the press try to be sneaky by disguising themselves as regular attendees by wearing regular attendee badges rather than press badges. In this instance, many exhibitors feel inclined to share potentially harmful or inappropriate opinions when prompted rather than guarding what is said. You should be careful to remind your sales team that, to the press, there is no such thing as an "off the record" conversation. Everything that you say could potentially wind up in a newspaper or a trade publication. For this reason, it is crucial to refrain from making derogatory comments about your competitors. Along that same line of thinking, you should never disclose any confidential information regarding your company or products. In fact, you should assume that, much like a Miranda warning, anything you or your sales team says could and will be used against you in the court of public opinion.

Another means of avoiding the unpleasant and potentially damaging trap of unwittingly speaking to a member of the press and divulging confidences is to qualify your prospects by asking them to tell you a bit about themselves before you give them your presentation. If this pre-qualification is not possible, however, you should apply the foregoing principal of keeping to the scripted presentation regarding the product or service that you are selling.

Gain Even More Exposure at the Show

Another powerful tool in the race to make the most of your exhibiting experience is to get your story published in the trade show's daily publication. You can get this additional jump start on your competition by contacting the newspaper editors a few weeks prior to the start of the show and asking if you could submit a story that might be of interest to them and to the public at large. Since one of the challenges of being in the publishing industry is finding worthy information to fill the pages of any given publication, including trade show dailies, you have a good chance of capturing that ever important publicity. As described in some detail above, the story should mimic the style and format of a well drafted press release. The information you submit should be concise, clear, and focus on the benefits that your company can provide to the trade show attendees.

You will note that the above-discussed methods for seeking pre-show and mid-show publicity were entirely free. From a purely fiscal standpoint, these techniques cost close to nothing yet can deliver $100's-$1000's of dollars in premium advertising. The human capital expended will more than pay for itself in later realized publicity and, ultimately, sales. By spending the time to create effective press releases and teaching your staff to properly deal with the press, your company's exhibiting experience will be tenfold what it would otherwise be. Don't miss the Bonus Section for more information on Paul Hartunian's Million Dollar System for publicity.

"A winner is someone who recognizes his God-Given Talents, works his tail off to develop them into skills, and uses those skills to accomplish his goals."

– Larry Bird, basketball player

Chapter 6 – Trade Show Promotional Materials

PREMIUMS – EXPOSING THE MYTHS

For the purposes of this chapter, I will assume that you have some experience on the trade show floor either as an attendee or as an exhibitor. Based on the foregoing, I can safely assume you have walked the trade show floor looking at the products and services that were of the most interest to you. If you remotely resemble the average trade show attendee, you likely walked up and down the aisles picking up the nice gel pens, the mouse pad, the rulers, and the cloth bags all emblazoned with the various logos and slogans that companies are trying to promote. Most often, the logos and slogans are nicely screened or printed on the items. With some confidence, I can assume that you picked up these expensive items and inspected the carefully thought out words. You may have even thought; "This Company really put effort and money into giving me something nice to take back to the office!" Now, I want you to think about what happened after you returned home or to the office, all your new trinkets in hand. How many of those promotional items ended up in the trash? How many are hidden away in a drawer somewhere never to see the light of day again? And, of course, the most important question; have you ever contacted a company and asked for their product information based solely on the information contained on any one of those nicely designed and well-thought out give-aways?

Don't Throw Your Money Away

Too often, exhibiting companies obsessively consider the kind of premium they will be giving away at a show. Their goal is to have the shiniest pen with the best gel covering or the brightest carrying bag crafted and stitched with the finest of fabric. The assumption, of course, is that this spectacular gift will draw the attention of every attendee strolling by. Far too often, the measuring stick used to gauge the success of the exhibit is the magnitude of the crowd that has paused to scoop up that special trinket that was so carefully thought out. When a long line of expectant attendees eagerly wait their turn to pick up the special gift being offered, the company perceives that as a sure sign of exhibiting success.

On the contrary, a vast majority of premiums lavishly expended on trade show attendees are nothing more than a great way to throw away that valuable and limited trade show budget. Although it seems the converse, in fact, it is extremely expensive and ineffective to have people standing in line at your booth for the sole purpose of collecting your premium. As alluded to, the existence of a stamped premium in an attendee's bag does not translate into a later sale. After all, how could that be the case? As you know from your own experience, attendees rarely look at the premium once it has found its way into that clever cloth bag purchased and distributed by another exhibitor. Unfortunately, trade shows are inundated with people who walk around on a mission to collect free stuff just because they can. Perhaps we can attribute this "hoarding" instinct to human nature or perhaps it is simply habit to take all that one can gather. Whatever the cause, one thing is certain: people do not purchase your product or service simply because you gave them that perfectly designed and expensive cloth bag nor will you leap to their mind when they need a product or service you offer just because their company's receptionist has a pen with your logo on it.

The Best Use of a Premium

Assuming you would like to incorporate a premium into your exhibiting experience, you should first consider what you want to accomplish by doing so. Do you want to incorporate your premium into your marketing message? Can you make the premium work for you by making it something that will encourage your prospects to buy? One approach some exhibitors use with respect to this issue is to send out a part of a premium to their best customers and most promising prospects as part of a pre-show marketing campaign. The premium itself can be used to encourage the recipients to stop by the company's booth particularly if there is an additional part of the premium that can be collected by all those who take the time to find the company's booth.

The best use of a premium, if you decide to use one at all, is to treat it as just that; a premium. Consider the connotation of the word itself. A premium is defined as a prize or award of superior quality or value. Of course, something that is so special should be reserved for the few people that you believe are important enough to receive it. The first group of people that should certainly receive a premium from you is your company's current customers. These are the people that buy from you already and have taken the time to come see you at the show. You should do everything possible to show them how much they are appreciated. Another group that should receive your premium are those prospects that have pre-set appointments with you in your company's booth. At the conclusion of the appointment, they should be rewarded with a memorable item. It should be something they would view as valuable. It should also be something that expresses your appreciation for their time and effort. Consider giving them an incentive to buy on the spot. For instance, the premium can be an exclusive sale for the next 30 days or a free upgrade to the product or service they are interested in.

Of course, you don't have to limit this practice to only

those that have made appointments with you before the show. If you find yourself engaged in a conversation with a prospect that you feel has the potential of becoming your company's customer in the future, consider rewarding them with a premium as well. If you decide to give them something tangible, then it should be something nice that they will keep and use. This requires a small investment on your part, but it may be worth it if it is only given out to your best customers and prospects. Consider a fountain pen, a day planner, or something more specific to your industry. For example, maybe you or someone in your company has written an interesting book on a topic related to your line of work. Giving a signed copy of it to your prospects and customers is a great way to show them that they are appreciated. One thing a premium should not be is something to attract a crowd to your booth. Those types of premiums rarely make the impact you are seeking. Instead, your premium should work as a marketing tool for your company for months and years to come.

LITERATURE

Whether you have exhibited at a trade show before or even attended one, you have certainly seen the next issue in action. Representatives of companies stand in front of their booths or their storefront handing out costly brochures and folders to anybody that meanders by whether they appear to have an interest or not. At a trade show, you can imagine that by the time an attendee has finished walking the aisles, he or she could have hundreds of pieces of promotional material to take home. Now, if you found yourself with a huge stack of brochures at the end of a show, would you ever consider taking all of that information back to the hotel or the office with you and sifting through it for hours on end to find the tiny gem among all those stones? Certainly not. The same is true of the lion's share of attendees. This is particularly true if the pieces take up too much space and are burdensome to carry. The shotgun approach with literature simply isn't practical nor is it cost effective.

You Wouldn't Give a Five Dollar Bill to Just Anybody That Walks By, Would You?

The next time you are at a trade show, you might want to conduct a little experiment. Walk around and look into the trash cans that generally line the perimeter of trade show floors. See how many shiny folders, binders and brochures are discarded just a stone's throw from where they were distributed. Too often, companies fail to honestly assess the effectiveness of handing out literature to every passer by. They mistakenly assume that getting their literature into the hands of attendees will result in sales. The reality, however, is quite the converse. Spending those advertising dollars on literature and then handing it out to every one that passes by is virtually the same as crumpling up dollar bills and slam dunking them into the nearest trash can. To be sure, the shotgun approach to handing out literature simply results in little more than lost capital.

The Best Way to Distribute Literature

Since over 90 percent of the literature that is handed out at trade shows never gets read, it is best to create a one-sheet informational piece that your staff can hand out at the show. These one-sheet handouts should be reserved for only those attendees that show some interest in your product or service.

This approach has the dual benefits of being relatively inexpensive and providing you a good opportunity to follow up with your prospects. For example, when you provide the prospect with your company's one-sheet informational piece, you can explain that a more comprehensive informational packet will be forwarded to them at the conclusion of the show. Then, if they show an interest, record their contact information on a lead sheet and make sure that your follow up material is timely mailed. This method is much more effective than handing out your expensive marketing material on the show floor where it is sure to be lost among the mass of competing flyers. Although you will have the added cost of postage, that expense is far less than printing up hundreds of extra binders.

While the foregoing one-sheet flyer should be your general approach to literature distribution at the show, you should also have a few copies of your expensive marketing folders at the ready. You should keep them hidden from public view and provide them only to prospects and customers who are anxious to get a more comprehensive look at your product or service right on the spot. As you have no doubt experienced, some prospects simply don't want to wait for a later mailed brochure. In that event, you shouldn't be caught empty handed, but rather, you should be ready with the materials on hand.

"It is the mark of an educated mind to be able to entertain a thought without accepting it."

– *Aristotle, philosopher*

Chapter 7 – Truth About Branding, Exhibit Design, and Signage

As a seasoned trade show veteran, I have made or been exposed to virtually every faux pas exhibitors make. While exhibitors are known to make widely divergent mistakes on the whole, I would like to draw your attention to three in particular. These mistakes are committed both by those well versed in exhibiting and by those new to the idea of trade shows. The first common mistake revolves around branding, which can be commonly defined as the process by which a trademark or distinctive name is developed to identify a product or a manufacturer. Next, there are mistakes with exhibit design. Exhibit design refers to the development of a layout, look, and feel for a display. Finally, companies often make mistakes in their use of signage – the manner in which words and phrases are chosen to represent a company's image. Let us now take a closer look at each one of these important topics.

BRANDING

As you know, bookstore shelves have no shortage of marketing books written on the subject of branding and, to be sure, each has its place. But, when preparing for a trade show, it is important to keep your priorities straight. The fact is, spending money on branding is a waste of valuable resources that can be used elsewhere. You, like all companies, are seeking the same goal. You want customers to buy from you time and time again. Branding is one way of facilitating that goal. However, you can certainly cultivate that repeat customer base before you establish a famous brand name for yourself.

Companies the likes of Coca Cola and Nike are able to afford to pump extraordinary sums of money into promoting their brand, but that doesn't mean that your company should follow suit. In addition to the very obvious name recognition they possess, these companies also have a solid following of customers who know and trust their products and services. Think about it. In fact, I would venture to say that most people don't purchase Nike shoes because they are emblazoned with the Nike logo or because Tiger Woods wears the famous swoosh on his golf shirt. It's because people know and trust the quality of Nike products that they are willing to shell out $80 for a pair of white sneakers. The actual brand name is secondary even though it has been ingrained into our culture and our minds. Had the founder of Nike decided to call her company by another name, the company would have nonetheless built its empire to the same level of success as they enjoy today.

The key to profitability in any business no matter how large or small is to concentrate on selling your product or service and to follow through on your promises. Only in this way can you establish the reputation necessary for success. By not only meeting but exceeding your customer's expectations, you will see that your brand will build itself. I think we can all agree that it matters very little, if at all, that a prospect recognizes your company name when they haven't an inkling about what your company has to offer. In fact, the really important thing is that your prospects learn they can trust your products and services as opposed to merely recognizing your name.

Of course, once your brand is established through outstanding service and support, having a recognizable brand name will certainly assist in growing your business to dizzying heights. Establishing your brand will create a stable position for your company in the marketplace. In addition, branding allows you to have price premiums and reduces the amount of competition you encounter. Your customers can rely on your brand name as a measure of their trust in you. Of course, establishing brand name recognition is only a valuable asset when you don't neglect those other vital areas of your business that will keep your clients coming back.

EXHIBIT DESIGN

As any trade show attendee knows, there are myriad attractive and exciting exhibits to be seen along the trade show floor. Unfortunately, that attractiveness comes at a cost. Indeed, most displays no matter how attractive are not designed properly for the trade show environment. Too many times, companies just copy their brochure, business card logo, or a magazine advertisement they have used and don't follow through on the basic rules of trade show exhibit design.

The cornerstone to a good display is a design that can capture a person's attention in three seconds or less. This is because attendees generally spend a mere three seconds scanning each display as they breeze by. This limited window of opportunity will close if your display isn't compelling enough to catch attendees immediately. Because you are so tightly restricted in terms of time, your display must be simplistic, yet appealing.

New exhibitors as well as seasoned veterans seem to fail equally at describing what their company does through signage and graphics. Time and again I have heard attendees asking an exhibitor's staff one small question that strikes at the heart of this issue: "What do you do?" If your company's booth is designed properly, nobody in your exhibiting team should ever hear that question being asked. Upon glancing at your booth, an attendee should immediately know the general category of product or service that you are offering. They should not be left staring at fancy graphics and pretty colors wondering what it all means. Large photographic images and bold headlines should properly convey your company's purpose to the attendee.

If, after looking at your properly designed exhibit, an attendee still does not understand what you can do for them, then chances are that the attendee is not a good prospect for your company. This ability to pre-qualify prospects based on whether they have an understanding of your business is yet another benefit of a properly designed exhibit.

SIGNAGE

Since a successful exhibit must convey what it is your company has to offer within three seconds, your signage must be clear and concise but sufficient to answer the most basic of inquiries. Despite what you may have heard or seen to the contrary, merely displaying your logo on the top panel of your exhibit is not enough. You and your team may know what your logo represents, but absent the branding discussed above, a trade show attendee likely has never heard of your company. Therefore, your logo is virtually meaningless to them.

The first step to successful signage is a carefully thought out word or phrase that unambiguously carries your company's message. Graphics and signage should be easily readable from 10-20 feet away. The size of the letters should be one inch in height for every three feet of distance from which the average attendee will be viewing your booth. As you can imagine, this large size does not allow for extensive writing, so the most important pieces of your marketing message should be prominently positioned for easy viewing. Since many attendees may be intimidated to stop in front of your booth, your key phrases and concepts should be big enough that they can be read at a glance without stopping.

"My father used to say to me, "Whenever you get into a jam, whenever you get into a crisis or an emergency...become the calmest person in the room and you'll be able to figure your way out of it."

– *Rudolph Giuliani, New York City mayor*

Chapter 8 – Trade Show Displays

TWO SCENARIOS

Imagine for a moment that you are an attendee at a trade show. You are walking down the aisle, canvas bag in hand, filled with all those brochures, feet beginning to ache when, out of the corner of your eye, you notice a colorful, exciting display. You stop and look from afar, noticing the modern-looking graphics, the flashes of color from the lights above, the strong angular look of the booth's protruding edges. You notice the name of the company emblazoned in large shiny letters along the top of the display but this is a company you have never heard of. The booth is a large space with lots of bells and whistles, but you notice that there are not a lot of people inside the booth except for a couple of booth staff. They have some gadgets on display in fancy cases, but by looking at them briefly you don't know what they are. Your co-worker, with whom you came to the show, catches up to you in the aisle and asks you what you're looking at. After a moment, you are embarrassed to say, "I have no idea!" The two of you then decide to just keep on walking along the aisle.

Now, imagine a different scenario. As before, you are walking the trade show floor, when out of the corner of your eye you notice a phrase that catches your attention. After all, you have been having problems finding an effective way to polish that darn widget back at your workplace and this company you've never heard of seems to be offering a widget-polishing machine that appears to be just what you were looking for! You stop to get a better look. Immediately, you notice that this particular display tells you everything you need to know about the company and the widget polisher. You see a professionally designed display with smart graphics and concise signage. Most importantly, you notice that there are bits and pieces of information that speak directly to your questions and needs. As you edge even closer to the booth, you notice a couple of smiling faces welcoming you, a nice space for professional interaction, and what looks like that very polishing machine that you've been looking for. Of course, you proceed directly into the booth for more information.

EQUAL OPPORTUNITY

Trade shows are a unique selling venue in that they afford smaller companies the same opportunities that bigger companies generally enjoy in the marketplace. At a trade show, potential customers can just as easily examine a small family-owned company's products as they can a large conglomerate's. In fact, smaller companies arguably have an advantage at trade shows because those large company representatives call on thousands of prospects every week. The trade show floor is a unique place for attendees to familiarize themselves with products and services that they otherwise wouldn't have had exposure to.

It is for this reason that your company's booth should accurately reflect your message to your prospects. As noted earlier in this book, you will likely find yourself next to and across the aisle from your competitors. If dozens of exhibitors are selling the same or similar widgets, how do you ensure that attendees stop to look at your widget first? Read on to learn the secrets that will tip the scale in your favor.

BOOTH SIZE

Unless your company is a major manufacturer with heavy machinery, you could probably get by with renting a small 10x10 booth to save money. The salient question, however, is what size booth will best accommodate and encourage your show goals? The size of your booth should be directly proportionate to your exhibiting goals. Your first task in determining how your show goals are going to be matched by your exhibit space is to consider what types of activities you will be conducting during the course of the show. For example, are you planning on carrying out demonstrations in your booth space? Will you be holding pre-scheduled appointments and therefore needing a small conference area? Is your goal primarily to attract large groups or individuals? Will you have a continuously running video presentation? Do you intend to display your company's products and, if so, will they require much space? How many people will be staffing your booth at any one time? Once you properly assess all of these issues, you will be able to determine which booth size is right for your company.

Calculating the Amount of Space Needed

Since booth space is very expensive at trade shows, and bigger is not always better, it is generally a much better practice to be conservative rather than aggressive when ascertaining what size booth will best serve your needs. You can get a fair estimate of the number of your potential visitors and, accordingly, the size booth that will be most effective for your needs, by using a simple formula. Using the stats provided by your show's management, simply take the number of attendees that visited 2 out of every 10 booths from past shows, which I call **SUSPECTS**. (If necessary, estimate a **SUSPECT** ratio of 50%.) Then multiply that number by the number of attendees who you feel should be highly interested in your offering and in visiting your booth (**PROSPECTS**). If show stats are unavailable from the management, then use 17% of your

SUSPECTS as an average. Divide your **PROSPECTS** by the number of hours in the show (**SHOW TIME**). This will tell you how many contacts (**LEADS**) your staffers should make in one hour. Since the average number of quality contacts that a staffer can effectively make per hour is 7, you now know about how many staffers are needed to properly run your booth.

Now estimate that you need an average of 50 square feet of space per staffer, and then add on the space that is taken up by your displays. You now have the total size that your booth should be.

SUSPECTS x PROSPECTS ÷ SHOW TIME = LEADS/hr

Sample Based on a show with attendance of 4500 people during a three day show with the exhibit hall open 4 hours per day.

SUSPECTS = Show Attendance X (50% of attendees that visit 2 out of every 10 booths from last show)

PROSPECTS = Number of attendees interested in your services (17% of your **SUSPECTS** as a minimum)

SHOW TIME = Number of hours exhibit hall is open.

LEADS/hr = The number of people you should expect to talk to each hour at your booth.

SUSPECTS x PROSPECTS ÷ SHOW TIME = LEADS/hr

(4500 x 50% = 2250 *SUSPECTS*)

(2250 x 17% = 382.5 *PROSPECTS*)

(382.5 ÷ 12 hours = 31.875 *LEADS/HOUR*)

(31 ÷ 7 = 4.5 *STAFF NEEDED*)

(4.5 x 50 = 225 square ft. of booth space plus your exhibit).

In the case above you would be looking at a minimum booth

space of 10' x 20' to a maximum of 20' x 20' space.

TYPES OF EXHIBITS

Once you have calculated the most appropriate booth size using the above formula, you can then begin to consider which exhibit configuration will best advance your company's exhibiting goals.

Tabletop Exhibits – Table top displays are most commonly used at smaller venues where exhibitors will generally all be exhibiting in a small space. A tri-fold shape is common for tabletop exhibits. Some even feature added lighting. You should make sure that your exhibit conveys your message in a clear and concise manner. It should look more like a billboard than a compilation of separate small posters. The benefits of tabletop exhibits are two-fold. First, they are very portable and, second, they are more affordable than their larger counterparts. Set up and tear down are extremely simplistic and can be accomplished by one person in a matter of seconds. The small size of a table top exhibit calls for no more than one or two booth staffers to be present at the show. That will be the case unless you are setting up several independent stations in a 20x20 booth space or larger.

Back wall Exhibits – Also called inline, or linear exhibits, these are the most common type of exhibit at a trade show. The back wall exhibit is a very effective backdrop for displaying your message prominently. Only one side of the exhibit is exposed to passers by. As a result, it is crucial that you make the most of the premium viewing space. The height of an average back-wall exhibit is about 90 inches. Whether you have a 10 x10, 20 x10, or a longer booth, you should be creative in how you arrange your exhibit so your exhibit will not get lost in the sea of other exhibits. Be careful not to create a barrier to your exhibit by blocking the front line with a table. Tables should be used sparingly and, when used, should be put on the sidewalls of the exhibit. You should strive to arrange your exhibit to create an inviting and welcoming tone. An inviting space naturally encourages attendees to step into your booth and examine your product offering. Again, your exhibit should display one cohesive message and look less like a bulletin board. As a general rule of thumb, two people can set up an average-size back wall exhibit in under an hour.

Island Exhibits – An island exhibit generally consists of over 400 square feet and is surrounded by aisles on all sides. Island exhibits provide a means to market your company's message with a four-dimensional approach. In addition, island exhibits provide much more area to work with than a back wall exhibit and far more area than a table top exhibit. There is usually enough space to set up separate functional areas within the exhibit such as a demonstration area and a conference area. As with the other two types of exhibits discussed above, the paramount concern is that your exhibit display one cohesive message to those attendees that step inside. With an island exhibit, you have the potential to capture more attendees' attention because they will be walking by your exhibit on all four sides. This allows for maximum exposure, but can create a challenge in making the exhibit accessible and easy to navigate. Large exhibits are great for companies who do a lot of trade shows and require a lot of space, but it is best if these large exhibits have the capability to be broken down into a smaller exhibit for other uses where such a large presence might not be necessary.

Peninsula Exhibits – These are similar to island exhibits in that they are usually at least 400 square feet in size. The obvious difference is that a peninsula exhibit has only three sides exposed to the traffic in the aisles. Even with less exposure in terms of aisle traffic, a peninsula exhibit nonetheless allows for sufficient exposure to attendees, while providing a back wall to act as the center of the exhibit. This type of design can be more navigable for attendees than the island style exhibit.

Cross-Aisle Displays – For those companies with a large trade show budget and a corresponding need for space, a cross-aisle display may be the best choice. These types of exhibits are almost certainly the largest and most impressive exhibits on most trade show floors. Such an exhibit takes up two separate spaces that span across an aisle thus providing an area where all attendees walk through the exhibit. Whether they look left or right, they will inevitably be looking at your products and your marketing message. This is a great tool to use to ensure that your company's desired prospects don't miss your presence at a show.

Remember to think through your desired exhibit type carefully before you commit to any one style. Just because your trade show budget may allow for a large display that does not necessarily mean that a large display is the wisest option for your company. You should thoroughly consider how your exhibiting goals can best be met when making this decision.

Starbucks® Effect

If, in fact, you decide that a larger, more expensive booth is right for your company, you may wish to consider yet another alternative. Instead of purchasing one very large 40x40 space on the show floor, consider breaking your booth up into two or four identical booths and spacing them out throughout the trade show. Just like a Starbucks®, your company will seem to be on every corner! Have several booths in spread-out locations throughout the show, make them look identical, staff them appropriately, and your company has multiplied its chances of attracting those visitors that the single location may miss. In addition, multiple exhibits convey a message of cohesiveness to your customers and prospects. They will be amazed that your friendly representatives seem to magically be everywhere on the show floor!

"He, who every morning plans the transactions of the day, and follows that plan, carries a thread that will guide him through a labyrinth of the most busy life."

-Victor Hugo, writer

Chapter 9 – Exhibit Design

In earlier chapters, we have explored the true purposes of exhibiting – name recognition, sales and lead generation. In light of the foregoing, it becomes clear that your display is just a marketing gimmick or show biz prop used to make prospects stop and talk to you. Accordingly, it is crucial that your display is designed in such a way as to attract a vast array of clients and prospects. In addition, the design of your display should be such that your staff can identify those prospects and potentials that are most likely to lead to sales.

The design and overall style of your exhibit will speak volumes to passersby. A company that appears at a trade show with a hand-lettered banner, a stack of brochures and some red hot candies in a beige ceramic bowl will soon find that attendees flow past without much more than a fleeting glance. While it is not necessary to invest a fortune in your exhibit, it is important to invest a sufficient amount in a professional looking display that will properly convey your company's image. By using some creative marketing techniques and creative exhibit design, smaller companies are able to create the same professional and successful image that larger companies generally enjoy.

DO IT YOURSELF

Pre-Made Displays

One option that companies have when buying a display is to forego the services of an exhibit design firm and instead order a pre-made display. This option should only be elected if your company knows exactly the style and content of the message your company is trying to convey. It is clearly not worth the marginal savings you will realize if your display ends up attracting the wrong kind of crowd or, worse, not attracting a crowd at all. If you have the expertise and skill to craft your marketing message without using the design services that many exhibit design companies offer, than you should feel confident ordering a pre-made display from an exhibit display company and adding the appropriate accoutrements once you have the bare display. Should you choose to purchase a premade display, you will find a number of companies with thorough websites showing the wide array of available exhibits. By searching the Internet or by looking through exhibit design catalogs, you can find a perfectly suitable backdrop in the form of a pre-made display upon which you can design the perfect advertisement for your company. If you are interested in a FREE design consultation see the Bonus Section at the back of this book for a FREE consultation. Our consultants will do the research for you and make recommendations. They do not work on commissions, so you need not worry about being sold something you just don't need. And always ask about our exclusive **365-Day Return Program.**

Don't Go for the Cheapest

Keeping the foregoing in mind, a word of caution is warranted before you consider ordering a pre-made display. A phenomenon has swept the industry; many companies are now offering dirt-cheap displays that are imported from lower-quality minded companies from other countries. That is not to say that all "Made in the USA" displays are without problems. While these lower quality displays look good to the eye, the problems arise from the use of inferior materials that quickly begin to deteriorate. It's true they still come with a lifetime warranty on the frame, which I might add is pretty much a standard in the industry, but you need to ask yourself, "Am I willing to eat the shipping cost if I need to return it to the factory for warranty repairs, plus the time and effort spent dealing with repair issues?" Another red flag item that should raise your eyebrows is if the unit comes with its own field repair kit. That seems to tell me a lot about what the manufacturer expects; it wouldn't be there if you are not gonna need it. I can honestly say there is only one pop up system that "in my opinion" is king. The manufacturer, "Classic Exhibits" boasts a Limited Lifetime Warranty against *normal use and abuse.* Now that is strong, but the best part is that in all the years I've represented their product, I have never had to return a single client's system to them for repair EVER. I wish I could say that about other manufacturers. So you can see if you are not diligent in selecting your pre-made display, you may find yourself in possession of a poorly made display that will require an extensive expense of time and money in the future. One of those hidden expenses is encountered in shipping the display back and forth to the manufacturer any time a part needs to be repaired or replaced. Since shipping is usually not covered by the warranty, your "bargain" display could end up costing you much more than a better quality display would have cost had you expended the extra money in the first instance. It is almost always the better choice to spend a bit more at the outset rather than deal with the expenditures inherent in purchasing a sub-standard display system.

Add Your Message

Assuming you decide to order a pre-made display, I recommend you choose a standard pop-up display. They are generally very easy to handle and lightweight. They come with fabric panels that are Velcro® friendly, facilitating your ability to affix and interchange graphics. Easy to affix signs and graphics ease aggravation during set-up and tear down. In addition, a lightweight display will be less expensive to ship. You can also choose to fill up the space on the display panels with oversized graphics that can be purchased from a printing company specializing in large format graphics designed to ship rolled and laminated for durability. The lamination will provide much needed protection against damage that generally occurs during repeated set ups and dismantles. Should you choose to embellish your display with graphics and images, they should be large enough to attract an attendee's attention at a mere glance. More importantly, however, your graphics should highlight a benefit to your prospects and customers rather than just focusing on your company name. You should be sure to use graphics that contain printing or a caption that explains the image to which it is attached. The company logo should not necessarily be the first thing that attendees notice; rather, attendees should be able to see your marketing message clearly. In fact, your intended marketing message should be prominently displayed at the top of your booth where attendees naturally look first.

Graphics Tips

As noted above, your graphics should be laminated and easy to transport. Avoid graphics printed on foam core or gator board, since these do not bend and often meet an early demise from excessive wear. In contrast, you can expect laminated graphics, which are easily rolled up and packed in a tube, to last considerably longer and be easier to use. Consider these tips that will help you save money on printing exhibit graphics:

- Use standard fonts and colors.

- Install hook Velcro® on the back of each laminated graphic panel so that they are easily interchangeable.

- Have your graphics designed to your liking before getting them printed, since changing your mind later can be very expensive.

- Make sure that at least two different people proofread your files for accuracy before approving them for printing.

- If your graphics include photos, take the photos yourself or outsource this task to a willing student.

- Design the graphics using such programs as Photoshop, Illustrator, or Freehand – you will be providing your printing company with an easier file to work with.

- Be open to cost-saving tips and suggestions from your printer.

USE AN EXHIBIT DESIGNER'S SERVICES

You and your trade show team may find that you are not comfortable taking on the exhibit design task yourselves. Many companies decide that they need some guidance when it comes to conveying their company's marketing message clearly. If you find yourself in this position and you do not know exactly how to go about choosing that perfect method for conveying your message in the most effective manner, I suggest using the services of an exhibit design firm. Such a firm, if picked correctly, will be an integral component of your successful exhibiting.

Selecting a Designer

Assuming you have chosen to outsource your exhibit design to an exhibit design firm, be prepared to encounter a vast array of exhibit design firms competing for your business. Just as in any other industry, the exhibit design industry has companies that vary in size, capability, price points, and other factors. Since ordering an exhibit will probably constitute a large portion of your company's trade show budget, it is important to make educated choices on whose services will give you the greatest return on this important investment decision.

Listen to the Opinions of Others

One effective method of sorting through the sea of companies that are qualified to offer you their trade show expertise is to explore various trade show floors as an attendee. As you scan the aisles, take extra care to examine the various displays you encounter. Write down what you like and what you don't like about the style, color, shape, design, size, signage and effectiveness of each display that catches your attention. Later, you can refer to this written list when considering what each company has to offer.

In addition, you or someone else in your company likely enjoys a close working relationship with other vendors or firms in your own industry or outside your industry that exhibit at trade shows. Take the opportunity to engage that company in a conversation about what they do and don't like in their exhibiting experience. This can give you a solid head start on things you might prefer when you begin the process of selecting the right company to help you craft your own exhibit. You can launch your investigation with the following questions:

- Is the display easy to assemble and take down?

- How many people does it take to operate?

- How long has it lasted so far?

- Have you had to deal with the manufacturer's warranty or repair department? How did that interaction go?

- Does the display have different panels that can easily be adjusted to fit the needs of different trade shows?

- Do you feel you got your money's worth out of the display you ultimately purchased?

- How easy was the exhibit design firm to work with?

- Did the design firm stay within your anticipated budget?

To further narrow down to the exhibit design firm you want to work with, you can consult your professional association for advice. Occasionally, the association will have a list of references for various design firms. Your association may be able to connect you with other companies that have used the services of these design firms.

What Services Do You Need?

The next thing to consider is what type of service you are willing to pay for. Many exhibit design firms are one-stop-shops. In addition to exhibit design and sales, they offer other much needed services such as budgeting, space selection, graphic design, storage, repair, staff training, and lead management. Depending on your company's size, needs, and trade show budget, you may choose to take on most of these additional tasks yourself. However, having all the loose ends tied by one company with the expertise to get the job done timely can be well worth the price you pay. Your trade show team should work together to assess the level of convenience you want versus the budget your company can afford.

Choose an Exhibit Designer by Interviewing

Once you have narrowed down your choices to three or four worthy candidate companies, you or a member of your team should put each of the candidates through a short, but valuable, interview process. You can be sure to select the company with which you will be most comfortable by asking them the following questions:

- What is their process for finding out your specific needs?

- What is their turnaround time?

- Do they provide graphic design services?

- Do they offer marketing support?

- What is their return policy?

- Do they offer free exhibit design assistance?

- Will they do a free rendering of your new display before you buy?

- Have they ever designed an exhibit for your industry before?

- What happens if you use your display several times but want to change it?

A Word of Caution

You should consider the following word of caution before settling on a design firm. You should assure, before signing that first check, whether your chosen firm clearly understands that the purpose of your exhibit is to tell a story and send your company's marketing message to a specific segment of the crowd. I raise this point because, unfortunately, many design firms simply don't understand that a trade show is the perfect place for direct marketing. They assume that your display budget should be spent on the best and the flashiest graphics and designs that appeal to a wide range of demographics, which waste time and money by requiring your staff to qualify each suspect in search of your real prospects. Firms that subscribe to this line of thinking often spend a company's entire exhibit budget on a cute and clever conversation piece often designed to brand your logo into the minds of the masses rather than on a display that will effectively reach your target market and improve your ROI.

SIX TIPS FOR EFFECTIVE EXHIBIT DESIGN

1. When shopping around for an exhibit, it is important to remember that price should not be the deciding factor

in your display decision. Of course, you want to stay as close to your budget as possible, but keep in mind that the trade show exhibit is an investment that will be used many times over. For example, if your company plans on exhibiting at just two trade shows per year, you can safely assume that a quality exhibit will last you at least five years. If your exhibit costs $10,000, that's roughly $1,000 per show – probably much less than booth space rental and travel will costs! You can see how factors other than price are very important in your choice of an exhibit. If you choose a lower-quality exhibit for a better price, you may find yourself having to refurbish your exhibit or buy a new one after just a few shows, which in the end generally causes more headaches and costs more money.

2. Your exhibit should be designed with various factors in mind. Remember, just as one size does not fit all, one standard look does not fit all, either. What will the function of your exhibit be? Do you want to attract attention, leave a good impression, facilitate learning, or do you have other goals? What message should an attendee get after looking at your exhibit for just three seconds? Are there size and other requirements that have to be followed according to the show manual?

3. One relatively simple and cost-effective way to enhance the look of your exhibit is to use appropriate lighting. It is no longer enough to rely on the bright overhead lighting at a trade show. In fact, exhibit manufacturing compa-

nies have many different options to choose from when it comes to targeted lighting. When used properly, lighting can enhance your product offering, create an impact, and draw people to your exhibit. It is important to note that some halogen lamps have been deemed unsafe to use at a trade show because they pose a fire hazard; your exhibit manufacturer should have the latest specifications. When planning the layout with your exhibit designer, make sure not to go overboard with the lighting. It should only be used where needed, and where it will serve a specific purpose, such as pointing out a feature on a product or drawing attention to certain keywords and phrases. Lighting can also be effectively used to guide the attendees to the demonstration area in your booth.

4. A somewhat new innovation in the trade show industry is the use of fabric. Instead of printing graphics and pictures on vinyl, your exhibit manufacturer should be able to suggest different fabric options to you. Usually, fabric is a cheaper and better alternative than vinyl. You also get an incredible sharpness of colors that you don't see on vinyl. Fabric has the added appeal of being easily washable and transportable while maintaining its durability.

5. If your company has exhibited in the past, you may already have an exhibit that could use updating or replacing. If it is time to retire your existing display, you should be careful to consider what you can salvage from it before disposing of it entirely. This is a good way to save those

valuable budgeted dollars. In fact, there is a good chance that you won't need to purchase everything new. Instead, your exhibit design firm should have a number of ideas on how you can re-use those old parts. It is very likely that the display is quite usable, at least for scavenged parts, unless it has been damaged by fire or water. Often, companies want to replace an exhibit because they feel the display is outdated as most companies evolve over time, leaving old styles behind in favor of more modern ones. That said, you should be aware that certain panels and support beams can be reconfigured to make a smaller exhibit instead of being thrown out completely. You can use your smaller exhibit at shows you feel don't warrant a large presence. Of course, you may still want to design and buy a larger, newer exhibit, but salvaging parts of your old one will give you greater flexibility in your ex-hibiting options.

6. Your exhibit, when completely set up, should create an open and inviting space for attendees to enter. It should be crisp and clean. Make sure to plan enough empty space inside your exhibit while creating plenty of hidden storage compartments for your supplies and your staff-ers' belongings. Any garbage should be disposed of out of sight immediately. Attendees generally avoid cramped and cluttered booths in favor of those with plenty of space to browse.

QUESTIONS TO ASK YOURSELF

There are certain questions that you and your team should ask yourselves when planning the design of your booth. Even if you find yourself working with a professional and friendly exhibit design firm, remember that it's always in your best interest to stay as informed as possible about the deciding factors that go into the design of your exhibit. This affects your bottom line and the effectiveness of your trade show efforts.

- The first thing you want to consider is what your display should accomplish. Your reasons for exhibiting should have been the first decisions made when you initially chose to exhibit. Based on your company's specific goals and objectives, your display should be tailored to your needs.

- How can your exhibiting budget be stretched to its maximum capacity? Could you possibly buy a used exhibit? Taking a used exhibit and adding personal touches to it can save a lot of money.

- What will attract your target customer? Do they want to see your product on display, or are they more interested in hearing about your company's new innovations? It's probably going to be a combination of both.

- Should your display be equipped with certain utilities? For example, do you need a water source for your product demonstration? By foreseeing such needs ahead of time, you will save money and not have to make any last-minute changes to the design of your exhibit.

EXHIBITS, NOT JUST FOR TRADE SHOWS

Too many companies treat their trade show exhibit like an old tuxedo carelessly hung in the closet for 364 days a year, seeing the light of day only for that once a year special occasion. On the contrary, your trade show investment dollar would be best served by considering other opportunities throughout the year where your display can be used.

For example, while you likely purchased your display so that you might travel to trade shows out of state, your company could also choose to hold its own marketing event in your offices or at another local venue. These local marketing events should incorporate the same planning and budgeting techniques as if you were preparing for a big trade show. Invite your customers and your prospects, and put on an event with which they will be impressed. This is a perfect place to set up your professionally designed display in order to convey your marketing message clearly.

The following are a few of the other opportunities for using your exhibit:

- Customer plant tours

- Meetings with investors

- New product introductions

- Community sponsorships
- Charity events
- Holiday parties
- Press conferences
- Sales training
- Business meetings
- Book signings
- Any other special event
- Don't forget your office lobby – it's useful storage

PUT YOUR EXHIBIT
TO WORK, ANY WAY YOU CAN

"Unless you are willing to drench yourself in your work beyond the capacity of the average man, you are just not cut out for a position at the top."

– J. C. Penney, retailer

Chapter 10 – The Importance of Training Booth Staff

Despite the changing global economy, one constant remains tried and true; people buy from other people. Trade shows epitomize this important concept in a way unlike most other venues. With the advent of the Internet and other forms of communication, it is very easy for a buyer to purchase a product or service from the comfort of their home or office. Why, then, do so many buyers spend their valuable time and money to travel, sometimes hundreds and thousands of miles, to trade shows and conventions? The answer lies in the simple human need for interaction. While it is true that some products and services have transcended the need for a person-to-person sales interaction, many more still require that personal touch. This is particularly true when big ticket items are at issue. Think back to the last big purchase you made, either personally or professionally, and consider whether you felt comfortable making that important decision absent the personal interaction with another person. Chances are, you appreciated the dialogue with the sales person that had the expertise to guide your buying decision.

In light of my earlier discussion that focused upon the importance of choosing the perfect display, I want you to consider the other component that will be equally important to your exhibiting success. Imagine that you expended a significant amount of time and energy in preparation of an upcoming trade show. You have engaged a design firm, created a colorful exhibit with attractive signage, purchased the perfect booth space in a strategically important location, shipped your booth to the show location to be set up by the union staff, when you suddenly learn that neither you nor your staff is able to attend the show in person. For the three days of the show, your professionally designed exhibit is there, your products are displayed, but your display booth is entirely vacant of personnel.

Now, imagine the opposite. You entrust your well-designed exhibit to a shipping company for transport to the show floor. Yet, something happens to your exhibit along the way and it never arrives at its destination or it arrives completely destroyed. Your capable staff arrive safely to the show but find themselves without a display to fill the booth space. Could your team nonetheless make a successful showing? Of course they could. Although an exhibit is certainly an important component of a company's trade show marketing plan, it is not the reason that attendees flood the exhibit hall aisles. If you have done your pre-show marketing and advertising correctly, your team should still be able to meet the company's show objectives, even if your display doesn't make it to the show.

It is undoubtedly true that your trade show staff is the most influential component of your exhibiting experience. On an average day at a trade show, a single booth staffer can influence more prospects' perceptions than an average salesperson can in an entire month. Consequently, it is crucial that your show staff be properly trained.

Since a trade show is the ultimate selling opportunity, your booth should be staffed with your company's top salespeople. If needed, you can help your salespeople relate to the benefits that they and the company will receive from successfully exhibiting at the show. Sometimes, your staff doesn't realize that dozens of their potential future customers are going to be stopping by the booth in the span of a few hours.

A good means of highlighting the importance of the exhibiting experience to your salespeople is to point out that trade show attendees have made a substantial investment in traveling great distances to attend the show and to investigate your products and services. This means that they are interested in not just the product or service but also in who is selling those products or services and how they are going about doing it. You should convey to your sales staff that trade shows provide the rare and valuable opportunity to give spellbinding presentations that will convince your prospects that they are making a wise buying decision in purchasing from your company rather than your competitors' companies.

On the other hand, you can clarify that trade shows are a good chance for your sales people to make a very poor impression on your prospects. By helping your sales people understand that they have a golden opportunity to make more contacts and talk to more prospects than they could in a month out in the field, you will ensure that they perform at the top of their game and make a positive and lasting impression.

CREATE A TRAINING MANUAL

Unfortunately, one of the most common yet fatal mistakes companies make is to fail to leave sufficient room in their trade show budget to properly train their staff. Thousands, if not tens of thousands, of dollars are spent on the exhibit, booth space, and transportation but the staff arrives at a trade show untrained and unsure of what to do. One means of avoiding this common mistake is to put together a training manual for each of your booth staffers. Once you have prepared such a manual, don't just hand it out expecting that your staffers will read and understand its contents. Instead, you should be sure to sit down with your team and highlight the important points that they should know. Your exhibit staff manual should contain, among other things, the following important information:

- Show hours, including setup and breakdown

- Hours that each staffer is expected to be present at the show

- Any after-hours events that require staffers' attendance

- A list and thorough description of each product that is to be displayed in the booth

- Pricing of the displayed products, and any at-show sales that will be held

- The goals of exhibiting, and what each staffer is expected to do to reach those goals

- The proper way to qualify prospects

- The presentation that each staffer is expected to give to prospects

- The lead handling process

STAFF INCENTIVES

Chances are your booth staff wasn't particularly excited about attending the show. Their regular duties are probably rather demanding and, from their perspective, they have been pulled away from what they are trained to do and thrust into an unfamiliar and sometimes unfriendly environment. If they are like most people, they are likely uncomfortable and unsure of what's expected of them. They are consumed with their thoughts of the work that is piling up on their desks back at the office. With a bit of effort on your part, you can teach them to understand the benefits of attending a trade show for both themselves and the company.

Not only should your staff be properly trained for the show, your staff should be rewarded for their participation in the show. Incentives are an effective way to motivate your booth staff. You can set goals for your team, being sure to make them attainable by as many of your staff as is practicable. Those goals can range from obtaining a certain number of qualified leads to selling a certain number of widgets. By creating these goals and making them attainable by your team, you can assure that hard work will follow.

Rewards and incentives for your staff can range from certificates of achievement to dinner for two at a local eatery. Incentives are especially valuable when the rest of your work force doesn't understand the time and effort that is expended in working a trade show booth. These incentives can also convey to your work force that attending a trade show is much more than a three-day vacation. Another incentive you can offer is to hold meetings where staffers recognize each other for something particularly well done at the show. Praise from peers has a high-perceived value to most workers and is a genuine way of building team spirit and respect.

INVOLVEMENT OF SALESPEOPLE

<u>Pre-Show.</u> To ensure a successful show, your staff should be heavily involved in the pre- and post-show marketing efforts. From the very earliest stages of planning, your team should be comprised of the people who will be present with you in the

company's booth. Brainstorming with your top salespeople on the most effective ways to reach your audience will give you an advantage over your competition. Divide responsibilities evenly among the members of the group, and make each person accountable for their assigned tasks. Not only will this make the job of planning for the show easier on you, it will also ensure that your salespeople share in both the workload and the benefits of exhibiting.

<u>Post-Show.</u> Your salespeople should also be involved in the post-show follow up. Too often, good leads go cold because they are left untapped in the aftermath of the show. As evidence of this phenomenon, you can perform a simple test when attending your next trade show. Spend time at many different booths, give them your business card, ask questions about their products, and then see how many of those companies actually follow up with you after the show. You will certainly be amazed at how few actually engage in hearty post-show follow up. Undoubtedly, as an exhibitor at a trade show, your team will have many qualified leads to follow up on. This is particularly true if you have done your pre-show marketing correctly. These leads can be distributed evenly among the staffers immediately following the show. This division serves two purposes. First, it assures that no one staffer will be left with the important task of following up with new leads. In addition, it can be presented as a reward for being productive at the show. In essence, you will be giving them pure sales leads that are usually easier to close than leads obtained in the field.

BOOTH ETIQUETTE

As you think about acceptable behavior for you and your staff at the trade show, *COMMON SENSE* should be your focus.

Consider the following **C.O.M.M.O.N.** sense points:

Control the interaction

You certainly don't want to overpower the prospect. In fact, you should use the 80/20 rule in your interaction with them. Speak only 20% of the time and allow your prospect to tell you valuable information about them 80% of the time. The point is for the salesperson to be able to guide the conversation while permitting the prospect to fill the conversation.

Open

Your Company's exhibit area must be open and clean. If you have planned for adequate storage space for such things as extra literature and personal belongings, there is no reason that the booth shouldn't stay clean throughout the show.

Maintain

A cohesive image of your company. Your booth staff should be wearing similar clothing. You can even consider providing them with a uniform. This uniformity presents your team as a united front and ensures that your staff is easily distinguishable from your competition.

Make

An effort to ask the right questions of your prospects. Since your average interaction with an attendee will only last three to five minutes, it is crucial to ask the right leading questions and listen carefully to the responses in order to make those crucial qualifying decisions. Make sure that the prospect does not leave your booth without committing to some sort of a follow-up from you.

Offer

Similar presentations to all qualified prospects. Based on the leading questions that your staff should be able to ask an attendee, the staffer should determine if the attendee is a good prospect or not. If they are, they should be given a short but informative presentation of your company's products or services.

Never

Eat, drink, or talk on your cell phone while you are in the booth. Each staffer should have a regularly scheduled break away from the booth in order to eat, rest, and do whatever is necessary for them to be re-energized.

Smile

A warm smile is the first thing attendees will see as they stroll past your booth. Setting the tone with a smile invites prospects to stop and talk with you. Your staff should always have a happy face on, no matter how tired or worn out they are feeling.

Eye

Contact. This habit is crucial in western culture. If you don't look your prospect directly in the eyes, they may think that you are not interested in them or that you are not telling them the truth. To come across as honest and trustworthy, your staff should maintain eye contact with your prospects throughout each conversation.

Name

You should instruct your staff to introduce themselves immediately when meeting prospects. Disabuse them of the notion that the prospect will read their badges upon that first meeting. Of course, the reverse is also important. Be sure your staffers take the time to read the attendees name, that is prominently displayed on their badges and address them accordingly. A greeting of "Hello Marianne, my name is John" will go a long way toward establishing a rapport with the attendee from the very start.

Show

Remember that attendees and other exhibitors can easily recognize each member of your staff even when they are not in your booth. Whether your staff is walking through the exhibit hall, or taking a break in the food court, they should act appropriately and always remember that they are still on stage and representing your company on and off the show floor.

Enforce

Proper body language with all your staffers. Their stance should be inviting and welcoming to the attendees. Crossed arms, standing too far away or too close and blocking your body with objects all send the wrong message to your prospects.

UNIFORMS

It is desirable for your Trade Show Team to portray a cohesive image on the show floor. A very effective method of creating that cohesive image is to supply your booth staffers with uniforms. This is true even if your office typically enjoys a very laid back and casual atmosphere.

Based on your desired company image, you have any number of choices with respect to uniforms or a dress code. You can choose to require your staff to wear business suits or you can purchase matching shirts with company logos on them. If you demand that your team wear their own business clothing to the show, make sure that you are very specific in what is appropriate and what is not. A dark suit may mean black for one team member and maroon for another. By specifying exactly what color and style of business attire is appropriate, you ensure a cohesive image for your staff.

One issue to consider when making this decision is comfort. Choosing polo shirts and khaki pants for your team may be a more comfortable solution than requiring business attire which can mean high heels for the women on your team. The point is to assure uniformity but to be cognizant that your team will be active for a good part of each show day. In addition, polo shirts emblazoned with your company logo are a great option if you have a large show team. Attendees can easily spot your salespeople and will be impressed by the amount of teamwork that the matching shirts imply.

UNWANTED VISITORS

If your company has exhibited at a trade show in the past, you have very likely encountered the following situation. A salesperson or a "consultant," or a solicitor from another company approaches you. They make their pitch to you in an effort to get you to talk to them about your business and about your company's need for their services. You realize that you don't wish to speak to them but you are also trying to be polite. You answer their questions, give them your business card, and before you know it you have spent a few minutes of your precious trade show time in an unproductive conversation. As they keep talking to you, you may even notice a prospect walking by out of the corner of your eye.

What do you do? How do you get rid of the unwanted visitor without seeming rude and inconsiderate? Most shows do have a "no solicitation" policy but many times this is not enough to keep the unwanted visitors out. They still manage to get into the show and attempt to take up the exhibitors' time and attention.

Your trade show team is the answer to resolving this unfortunate situation. Prior to the show, you and your team should anticipate this scenario and discuss ways to resolve it. If a polite "No, thank you" doesn't seem to be effective, you should instruct your team to use some sort of a secret sign that conveys your need for assistance. Upon seeing the sign, team members can politely excuse one another from the unwanted interference. In this way, you can keep the focus of the show on making those precious contacts with new prospects rather than waste that trade show floor time in an unproductive situation.

THE IMPORTANCE OF TEAMWORK

Interaction with prospects generally consists of elements that are quite the same irrespective of the underlying product or service. If a widget-cutter client exists out there, then he must be one out of a million or more. By definition, he is then no longer a widget-cutter client, but a unique individual just like the rest of us. When a hundred prospects each look at the same widget, you would think that they would be able to come up with very diverse questions about the widget. How does it interact with my current widget? How much noise does it make? Will it run with my current software program? Can it be shipped to an alternative location for the same price? You get the idea. You might have thought that the list of questions could be endless. Interestingly, that isn't the case. The same questions tend to arise over and over despite how diverse your potential clientele. Nonetheless, you will get that odd ball question here and there for which you will need to prepare as best you can.

You and your team should set aside time before the show to ensure that each member is properly trained to answer questions about your products and services. But, as you encounter those unexpected questions that are sure to arise, this is where teamwork becomes very important. It is wise for each staffer to know the strengths and recognize the weaknesses of the other team members. Then, as an unexpected question comes up, the salesperson can feel comfortable in redirecting that question to the person in their team that is best suited to answer it. Everybody wins when teamwork is evident, and most importantly, the customers' wants are met.

As attendees stop at your company's exhibit, you are sure to encounter the question "Tell me a bit about your company." Your entire show team should feel completely comfortable in answering this question briefly but effectively. Make sure that your staff understands your company's marketing message, which should also be evident in your booth design. Upon glancing at your exhibit, examining your products and hearing a brief statement about your company from your staff, the attendee should be left with one cohesive message that is easy to understand and easy to remember.

It is also important to thoroughly review your exhibiting goals with all members of your staff. As discussed in the beginning of the book, your goals should be clearly defined and written down. Don't just hand a copy of your show goals to each salesperson and assume they will read and understand them. Make sure to go over each point thoroughly ensuring that all your staff is on the same page. If, for example, one of your goals is to generate sales while at the show, the last thing you want your staff doing is trying to set up sales appointments for after the show.

Each member of your staff should know exactly what is expected of them before, during, and after the show. Go over the schedule with the team, making sure that your booth is staffed with enough people at all times. Inform your staff ahead of time that additional hours may be necessary, for example, when you're setting up your booth or entertaining clients and prospects after hours. Each staffer should be crystal clear on their responsibilities during the show. One effective way to achieve this level of understanding is to create a simple trade show trivia game consisting of what's expected of them at the show.

CONCLUSION

By now, you understand that one of the main reasons that attendees take the time to travel to trade shows is to get a chance to personally interact with company representatives. The staff that you choose for your booth will be acting as the face of your company for the two or three days of the trade show. The cost of staffing your booth with untrained people can be devastating.

For this reason, it is crucial that each staffer is properly trained and is fully aware of what is expected of them while at the show. Don't make the mistake of assuming that just because your staffers are top salespeople in your organization and are proficient in selling to your customers out in the field, that they will be able to automatically transfer those skills to the trade show environment. On the contrary, those staffers who are excellent at their everyday job may have a hard time adjusting to the unique environment of the trade show. To make the trade show a success, and to get the most out of your trade show budget, you should remember to thoroughly train your staff before and during the show.

"There are no real shortcuts to
any place worth going."

– Beverly Sills, opera singer

Chapter 11 – Lead Management

LEAD SHEET CREATION

At most trade shows, exhibitors have the option of renting a lead processing unit that makes it easier to collect attendees' information. While this can be an effective way to gather some information about your prospects, beware of relying on the machine to give you all of the information you need to know. The lead-processing machine gathers only the attendee's basic information such as the attendee's name, company and company address. However, what you should be collecting is a detailed, customized profile of each of your prospects.

By creating a lead sheet and making sure that it is followed closely with each prospect interaction, you ensure that all vital prospect information is captured. The lead sheet should be put together based on the recommendations of your trade show planning team, which, of course, is made up of your top salespeople. Your salespeople know what information is important to them when making sales calls. Accordingly, you should use that resource when considering what information you want to capture on the lead sheet. Once all pertinent questions have been compiled into a lead sheet, you should have them prepared and at the ready for your trade show. After each transaction with a prospect, your sales team should then fill out the lead sheet by hand. Fully completed lead sheets will greatly enhance your post-show marketing efforts.

Another helpful way to manage your leads is to establish a ranking system that permits your sales team to indicate a prospect's purchasing potential. For example, a prospect that is very interested in your product or service would be ranked a 1, a prospect that indicated a strong interest but isn't prepared to purchase your product or service until sometime within the next year would be ranked a 2, and an attendee simply indicating an interest for some unknown future purchase would be ranked a 3. Of course, this ranking system should be customized to your product or service such that it will best accomplish your company's exhibiting goals.

The lead sheet should also facilitate proper follow-up with prospects. As with all good sales people, your booth staffer should conclude each interaction with a specific request for that next contact. Your salesperson should be sure to detail with the prospect what to expect as well as clarify on the lead sheet how your company is expected to follow up after the show. Does your prospect want to receive literature from your company in the mail? Have they asked that a representative call them to discuss the product or service further? There should be a separate space on the lead sheet to record the follow-up activities that the prospect is expecting.

Very often, exhibitors merely collect attendees' business cards as the lead sheet. Some even attempt to frantically scribble cryptic information on the back of the business card in an effort to remind themselves later who each prospect is and what they want. This is undoubtedly the wrong way to collect leads. A business card simply does not provide enough space to gather all the critical information you will need for that later follow up. And, even if you manage to find the space to write down that the prospect wants to talk to you on the phone following the show, partial information scrawled on a business card impedes your ability to organize those valuable leads after the show. This is not to say that you should throw away all business cards that attendees hand to you as soon as they walk away. Instead, you should provide your sales team with a stapler so they can staple the business card to the corner of the lead sheet they just filled out. This gives your team even more information on the prospect such as the proper spelling of their name and their direct line. The following is an example lead sheet that you can copy or modify for your specific needs.

Make Your Next Trade Show Pay...Not Cost!

SAMPLE LEAD SHEET

LEAD SHEET

Show Name _____   Date _____

Consultant _____

Prospect Name   _____

Company   _____

Address   _____

City, State, Zip _____

Phone   _____ Cell _____

Fax   _____

Company Profile _____

Identifying Characteristics_____

Prospect Ranking (1=hot, 2=warm, 3=cool)   1   2   3

Details_____

_____

_____

Product Interest _____

Need for Product _____

Role in Buying Process _____

Interest in Buying _____

Buying Time Frame _____

Estimated Budget _____

Expecting Follow-up (check any):   _____Mail Literature _____Date

                                              _____Personal Call   _____Date

                                              _____Other   _____Date

Post-Show Follow-up:
    1. Date_____   Result_____

    2. Date_____   Result_____

    3. Date_____   Result_____

    4. Date_____   Result_____

    5. Date_____   Result_____

LEAD SHEET MANAGEMENT

After reviewing a number of surveys and observing the behavior of countless sales people at trade shows, it is clear that most attendees walk away from the show feeling that their needs have not been met. Generally, this is the fault of the booth staff rather than the attendee. For this reason, booth staff should be thoroughly trained in being able to identify the attendees' needs and wants.

As attendees approach your company's booth, your staff should be asking questions such as "What prompted your interest in our product?" rather than generically saying "How may I help you?" The questions and answers that follow the initial introduction should focus on the information that you're looking to collect from your prospects. For example, your staff will realize a much greater level of communication with the prospect if they ask questions that will reveal what needs the prospect has that your company might be able to fill. Along that same train of thought, your team can ask the prospect what he or she likes or dislikes about the product they are currently using. Another good question to consider asking is how soon your prospect is thinking about making a purchasing decision. While these questions strike at the heart of what a prospect needs, your team should also try to learn what your prospects want. What a prospect needs and what they want are often two entirely distinct things. As we know, people are often more inclined to spend money on something they want as opposed to something they need.

The foregoing questions are vital to an effective post-show

marketing strategy. At the instant that your salesperson concludes his or her conversation with a prospect at the show, he or she should fill out the lead sheet in its entirety. It is not wise to rely on one's memory, as memories tend to fade quickly, particularly when the subject of that memory isn't emotionally charged. After speaking with two or three consecutive prospects, your salesperson will likely forget the details of previous conversations. Distractions abound in a noisy trade show hall. Those distractions could mean the difference between an effective follow up and one that falls far short of its mark. While it takes a minute or two to write down all of the details and check off the appropriate boxes, those moments are indeed money in the bank. For one company, I used my experience in creating magical props to build a magical clipboard of sorts. We had a digital recorder secretly built in to the clipboard, which allowed our clients to record accurate information on each prospect with just the touch of one finger. Now, instead of counting on their memory or the notes that commonly end up as little more than chicken scratch, each interview was recorded as its own searchable audio clip. We call this our **Magic Data Board 2000** and we still get requests for these units today. If interested, just give me a ring. The next model will feature up to 40 hours of recording time and is expected to be half the size of the older versions.

As is clear from the foregoing discussion, all companies should use a lead sheet along with the lead generation machine. By cross-referencing these two pieces of information on an attendee, you will have a complete profile of your prospect.

Of course, it is critical that each member of your sales team is thoroughly trained in the use of both the lead generation machine and the hand written lead sheet. As an added measure of training, you should gather your sales team and conduct a dry run on capturing leads. You can act as an attendee and have each staffer interact with you. They can then practice proper lead compilation and you can assess any areas that need special attention. Only when your sales team is completely comfortable with this lead compiling process will they be able to smoothly perform in a crowded trade show hall.

LEAD MANAGER

Since it is so important to collect the right information on your prospects, you would do well to designate a person in your booth to be the lead manager for the team. This person should be responsible for collecting the lead sheets and making sure that they are properly stored. As shocking as it may sound, there have been many occasions where I have managed a show for a client and found a box overflowing with those money-making leads discarded in a valueless heap next to the garbage can. Many companies forget to designate a person responsible for retrieving the leads and bringing them back to the office. Since virtually every company is seeking to use the trade show as a lead generation tool, leaving those leads at the show renders the time and money spent meaningless. Of course, assigning a lead manager and making sure they do what they're supposed to requires a great deal of organization and teamwork. Each member of your staff will have to regularly turn over their completed lead sheets to this designated person. By having a central point of contact for all of your lead sheets, however, you ensure that no information falls through the cracks and gets lost in the hustle and bustle of a busy trade show. Here at www.capitalcityexhibits.com clients often have us assist with the set up and dismantle of their exhibits. On many occasions, we have found ourselves in the position of rescuing our clients' lead cards or business cards. I believe that is a direct result of the company failing to designate a lead manager responsible for collecting the leads. Each member of the team believes that another member of the team was making sure the leads were secured. You can easily avoid this grave mistake by making the proper designation of a lead manager.

"Long-range goals keep you from being frustrated by short-term failures."

– James Cash Penney, retailer

Chapter 12 – Effective Presentations and Hospitality Events

PRESENTATIONS

As discussed in chapter 10, your booth and your staff are key elements in the image your prospects will see. You can enhance that image and draw more qualified leads if you retain an experienced presenter to hold an interactive presentation in your booth. A good presenter can even identify targeted prospects for your sales team to interact with both during and after the presentation.

Set the Stage

Whether you have a small 10x10 booth or a large island exhibit, before you engage a presenter or even choreograph a presentation that will be presented by your own staff, you should consider the type of presentation you would like to conduct in your booth. Irrespective of the size of your booth, you should have a stage area from which the presentation will be conducted. Having a small raised platform will set your presenter apart from the attendees and typically attracts other attendees over the course of the presentation. The goal in having a presenter is to attract and stop a greater number of attendees than you would otherwise draw.

Of course, the size of your booth will partially dictate the size crowd you are able to accommodate. Depending on the size of the booth and the audience you anticipate attracting, it is generally a wise investment to rent or buy a wired or wireless headset microphone. In my experience, wired microphone sets afford far higher voice quality than wireless sets do, but the trade off is more difficulty in set up and teardown. If you decide that a wireless set best suits your needs, make sure that you have a wired microphone on hand in case of a malfunction. If your presenter is not a hired professional, you should have your presenter practice using the microphone until he or she is completely comfortable with it.

Presentation Tips

Ideally, your company should have scheduled presentations at regular intervals. For example, your presentations could be slated for every hour on the hour. When using this type of repetitive presentation style, you should be sure to display a prominent sign in the booth clearly indicating the schedule of presentations. When using a presenter, less is more. The presenter should speak for just a few minutes and make the presentation as interactive and lively as possible. Attendees are generally making an effort to see many exhibitors and won't stay put for long. Capturing their attention for a few moments will be more than enough to get your message across and get the information you want.

If at all possible, try to avoid using videos during your presentations. Attendees tend to be more drawn to live people giving interesting presentations than they are to static videotapes. The presentation should focus on the benefits of the product or service to your customers. If possible, you should include as much audience involvement as possible. Incorporating audience involvement can be easily accomplished by having them pass an item around so that everybody can get a closer look or ask them to repeat a "magic" word. Attendees interacting with your presenter are often more engaged than those that are simply observing.

The presentation should be tailored in such a way that you can identify what prospects appear to be interested in your product or service as opposed to those that aren't. By asking certain questions of the audience and by discussing things that are important to potential clients, you almost ensure that those who are interested will stick around after the presentation. At the end of the presentation, be sure you have additional salespeople on hand to answer questions from the audience.

Your exhibit staff should be thoroughly trained in all aspects of your product or service so that they can effectively handle any questions your audience may raise. Exhibit staff should also be trained to ask the right questions of the attendees to determine if they are good prospects or not. Is the attendee the decision-maker for purchasing products for their company? When do they plan on making their purchasing decision? Does their company have a need for your product or service? Remember that a good presentation will give you an opportunity to connect with more qualified prospects at the show.

A Time and Place for Videos

Earlier I commented that you should elect to use a live presenter rather than a video. My recommendation in this respect stems from the idea that video presentations are often less effective than a live presentation because they cannot be as personal and interactive. That said, I do believe there is a proper time and place for their effective use. In fact, when used correctly, they can be a powerful and cost effective tool. If you find that you have a video you think could add to your exhibit, I suggest keeping it brief. A brief video can retain a prospect's interest if you are tied up in another conversation and there are no other team members available. If you find yourself in this situation, you can briefly interrupt your current conversation, quickly introduce yourself to the new prospect and offer them a short video to watch while you wrap up your conversation with the first prospect. This way, you don't lose the attention of a potentially valuable customer, nor do you alienate the customer you are already engaged with. A video can also be an effective grabber if it contains a celebrity or celebrity look alike. But use caution when taking this approach as you don't want to run afoul of any law prohibiting the use of another's likeness in a commercial setting.

PRESENTATION TECHNIQUES – BEGINNING TO END

Opening

Many times, out in the field as well as at a trade show, a salesperson will inadvertently be making a sales pitch to the wrong person. By "wrong person" I mean that the recipient of the sales pitch may not be responsible for making any buying decisions for their company and just happened upon your booth in search of information. Likewise, perhaps that person and their company will never be in the market for the goods or services you have to offer. Without properly identifying the prospect first, the salesperson may be foolishly wasting valuable time by jumping into a presentation that can never result in a sale. Such a shotgun approach to sales often dampens a company's trade show success.

As mentioned earlier, it is critical to train your sales team in the proper prospecting techniques before launching them into a trade show setting. By asking the right questions, the salesperson should be able to narrow down the sales potential of any attendee. A corollary benefit of asking good questions is that the answers to those questions can guide your salesperson on the type of presentation that would be most effective for that particular prospect. For example, an engineer may benefit from receiving more technical information on your product than a purchasing manager would.

Trade shows by nature only afford your sales team a limited window of opportunity to speak to people about your product or service. This limitation literally forces your team to narrow their questions to only those that matter most. Although only you and your trade show team can determine which questions are most appropriate for your company, I would like to provide a few examples of opening questions for your consideration:

- What product/service do you currently use in your company?

- Who in your company helps you make the purchasing decisions?

- What key features are you looking for in a product/service?

Middle

Once your salesperson has been able to determine the viability of the prospect and their most basic needs and desires, it is time to move on to the presentation. As you have already learned, the presentation should be short, educational, and as interactive and entertaining as possible. The trade show floor is fast paced and attendees have only so much time and patience before they begin to tune out. For this reason, your presentation should incorporate asking those key questions of your audience.

Whether you have an audience of one or five or more, by asking the right questions you will be engaging your audience, keeping their attention and interest, and also gathering vital information that will help you sort through the viable leads from those that simply aren't in your market. If you are presenting to a small group, have a second team member on hand to assist you. As you ask those key questions, your assisting team member should be collecting the bits of information that will help guide you in your effort to qualify your audience. At the conclusion of your presentation, you will have a completed lead sheet on each prospect and you will have a much clearer picture of what their needs are.

Here are some questions I have seen used effectively in the trade show arena. Of course, you should tailor these questions to meet the specifics of your product or service:

- What concerns do you have regarding the use of this widget?

- What do you think of this widget's performance?

- By show of hands, how many of you have had an issue with another widget's performance?

Closing

Once the salesperson finishes making a presentation to a prospect or a group of prospects, you should then move on to the proper closing questions. Remember, it is vitally important for you and your staff to pay close attention to what your prospects say. The 80/20 rule is one to live by, especially in a busy trade show setting. Your staff should be speaking only 20% of the time and listening to what your prospects have to say the remaining 80% of the time. If you give them a chance, your customers and your prospects will tell you exactly what they want from you and what obstacles, if any, stand in the way of them choosing to purchase your product or service. By gleaning information from what your prospects volunteer, you can better tailor your continuing interaction with them following the show.

As all good sales people know, closing the deal is as important in many respects as finding the right prospect to engage in your presentations. Both parties should walk away from the conversation knowing exactly what the next step in their interaction will be. To that end, you should ask your prospects the following types of questions as you wrap up your conversation with them:

- When do you plan on making a purchasing decision?
- How soon can we contact you after the show?
- Should we also contact anybody else in your organization?

Presenting to Clients

If you have done your pre-show marketing properly, you will surely have a healthy number of pre-set appointments with clients and prospects in your booth. These are people that you likely pre-qualified well in advance of the show. If they are already your clients, then simply pulling their file and jotting down key information about them before the appointment will give you an advantage in your meeting with them. As is true with all people, your clients want to feel welcome and important when they come to your booth. You can easily satisfy this desire by spending a bit of time in pre-show preparation.

Presenting to Prospects

In cases where the pre-set appointment is with a prospect rather than a current client, you can nonetheless prepare in advance. When making the appointment, ask the prospect detailed questions about their company. Then, do a quick Internet search in order to learn all you can about other information they might not have shared with you. Your prospect will be duly impressed with the details that you know about their organization. At the same time, this knowledge will give you an opportunity to ask them more focused questions that will assist in your further interaction with them.

Be Prepared to Present

That said, it is of paramount importance not to overwhelm attendees with too many questions or too much information. The line between bombarding your prospect with question after question and launching into a rote presentation without sufficient information is fine at best. This tightrope act is yet another reason to carefully train your staff before you unleash them on unsuspecting attendees. The fine line your sales team will be walking can be steadied by a fast paced, entertaining presentation style. This type of approach will alleviate a multitude of errors as the attendee will soon be engaged in the presentation and forget about any faux pas committed at the outset. As a team, you should write down guidelines for interaction with attendees, and make sure they are followed each and every time.

Also important is dress rehearsal of the presentation by all the team members assigned this task. As a professional performer for the last 40 years, I have learned how valuable this particular tool can be. In advance of any performance, I rehearse my presentation in great detail both mentally without a single prop in my hands and later with the actual equipment I will use to dazzle my audience. In this critical rehearsal period, I identify blips in the performance that, if left unchanged, would slow the pace and result in a less than exciting final product. The same is true with your team. Rehearsal steadies the nerves and identifies potential problems before they are played out in front of your prospects. This pre-show rehearsal can culminate in an at-show rehearsal where your team can stand in the booth and perform the well-choreographed presentation you have prepared. This will set the stage for a flawless show and a high return on your investment.

DEMONSTRATIONS

It may surprise you to learn that many attendees also engage in pre-show preparation. They commonly conduct their own research about the companies they intend to visit and will be well versed in your product or service. In this age of the Internet, they have ready access to online information that will enhance their understanding of what you have to offer before you have the chance to pitch it yourself. Once they embark upon the show floor, they are generally ripe and ready to see your products and services in full living color. In fact, the Center for Exhibition Industry Research conducted a study in which it found that 28 percent of attendees were drawn to those exhibitors who conducted a live demonstration in their booths.[1] Because attendees are anxious to see the newest widget in action, it is well worth the effort to include an in-booth demonstration along with your presentation.

Naturally, people are drawn to a scene where something exciting is happening. Movement of parts, noise, lights, laughter, or any commotion for that matter will generate more interest in your booth. Following an effective demonstration, particularly one in which your audience is brought to laughter, prospects walk away with a distinct memory of what they have seen and how it works. With particularly effective demonstrations, attendees may even recount the experience to others back at the office! Remember, trade SHOW is two words, with each being equally important to your success.

Cost-Effective Method

Consider how a product demonstration is beneficial to exhibitors in other ways. Conducting a demonstration provides you the rare opportunity to showcase the features of your product in front of dozens, if not hundreds, of prospective customers in just a few days. If the product demonstration had

---

1   July 1982 "Trade Show Bureau Research Report #13."

to be done individually with each prospect at their place of business, or even on your company's premises, you would be required to spend far more time, money and resources than is required for an in-show demonstration. By capitalizing on the unique nature of a trade show, you can reach a far larger audience with a fraction of the out of pocket expense you would otherwise spend to reach the same number of prospects.

Effective Demonstrations

Unfortunately, I have seen live demonstrations fail and fail miserably. The reasons for this painful experience are far too numerous to recite here, but the most common are as follows: the demonstration lasts too long, it doesn't convey the company's main marketing message, it is boring, or it wasn't properly rehearsed and doesn't flow as it should. To be effective, you should engage a professional who is completely comfortable with what's expected of him or her. A professional in this context doesn't necessarily mean a hired gun. You may have someone right in your own office who is sufficiently versed on performing and handling a crowd to be just perfect for the job. While some companies are fortunate enough to have that perfect person already on staff, most often this just isn't the case. In that event, your money would be well spent on hiring a person who can carry a live demonstration and leave that positive lasting impression you are driving for.

Imagine this: you assign John the task of giving the demonstration because he is the most gregarious fellow in your office. He is quite comfortable in front of all your office staff and never lets an opportunity pass to get in a funny word.

Now, here he stands in front of your target audience, widget in hand, pale as a ghost and dryly reading from the card fluttering nervously in his hand. In a matter of moments, you can be assured that crowd that had gathered at the sound of your intro music is disappearing right along with John's confidence. The person conducting your demonstration must be lively and entertaining. He or she must engage the crowd and be ready to handle any off the cuff remark shot from the crowd. At the same time, that person must be competent at weaving your marketing message throughout the demonstration without making it seem like a full blown commercial. In the event you draft the script for your demonstration, you should limit the points made to no more than three. This will keep the ball rolling and the audience engaged.

As mentioned before, your presenter should also make a concerted effort to involve the crowd in the demonstration. Whether it is asking someone to hold something up for everyone to see, or dropping their card in a fish bowl, crowd involvement almost ensures that attendees will stay around for the whole presentation.

Practice Makes Perfect

If you have decided that John, your employee, is qualified for the job of demonstrating your product or service at the show, you should ensure that he spends ample time practicing in front of others. Your presenter must understand every aspect of how your product works and must be able to relay that information to attendees without boring them to tears. Having your in house presenter start practicing in front of your trade show team well in advance of the show will result in a far higher quality presentation. Also, it is a good idea to have your team briefed by your presenter with a mock run-through of the demonstration an hour before the show opens on the first day. In the event you have engaged a professional presenter, you won't need as much pre-show preparation. This person is quite accustomed to working a crowd and should be prepared without your direct supervision.

At the risk of discounting the value of physically practicing your presentation, I want to emphasize the importance of mental rehearsal. As mentioned above, mental rehearsal is equally if not more important than physical rehearsal because it is the only means of performing perfectly every time. Countless studies have been conducted on this very issue. In those studies, subjects are divided into two groups. One group is permitted to practice the activity with physical props in hand while the other is restricted to mental rehearsal. In those studies, the mentally rehearsed group almost always outperforms the group that was permitted to practice the activity with the item. This has been attributed to the value of practicing perfectly every time. When you actually get to the venue, your performance largely parallels your practice and, as we all know, perfect practice makes perfect performance.

HOSPITALITY EVENTS

Depending on your industry and your company's experience with trade shows, you and your colleagues may have been invited to various private hospitality events. These private events are typically held by companies and reserved for their best clients, prospects, and vendors. For companies holding these events, they provide a great opportunity to network with those people and organizations that are vital to their success. For those invited to these events as attendees, these events provide a one on one opportunity to discuss the newest products and services offered by the hosting company. If you plan and execute a hospitality event correctly, you will enjoy the one on one attention from your guests that leads to a longer and more profitable relationship. In addition, these events can set you far apart from your competition.

Pre-Show Marketing of Your Event

A major consideration in your pre-event marketing strategy is how to ensure that your event is well attended by the right people. One means of achieving this goal is to mention the event in your pre-show communications with prospects and clients. Don't give out every detail of the event; rather just try to pique their interest by mentioning your decision to host such an event. Then, as you or a designated member of your staff talks to your prospects and clients in advance of the show, you can discuss the hospitality event in more detail. By personally extending an invitation to your best clients and your most promising prospects, you increase the likelihood that they will make the time to attend the event.

You can also encourage those special attendees to stop by your trade show booth and pick up their personal invitation to the hospitality event. That invitation should be the first time that your prospects and clients get all of the details they need to know about the event: the when and where. This serves the dual purpose of ensuring that only invited people will attend your event, as well as ensuring that your best clients and prospects don't miss your booth while attending the trade show.

A Hospitality Event is a Business Function

A hospitality event is generally held in a large hotel room or a reception hall. They are fairly upscale events, in turn making them more exciting to attend. If a company has the desire to be more creative, they can arrange to hold the event in a more unusual venue such as a zoo or another place of entertainment. While this unusual setting can be interesting, you should keep in mind that the event should be easily accessible by all of those attendees who are from out of town, as most of them will be. You should plan your event as a business function as opposed to a social event. These types of events are commonly held in the evenings after the show floor closes so you will probably want to incorporate food and drink. You should also convey the importance of this special event to your team members and make their attendance mandatory. The dress code should be consistent with your designated show dress. Remember, your prospects and clients will be evaluating all aspects of your company's image and it is important to maintain a professional decorum at all times.

Use the Hospitality Event as Another Marketing Opportunity

As with all other aspects of your trade show preparation, you must maintain your marketing message as a central focus. Although it may be well received by your guests, it is not enough to just invite customers and prospects to an open-bar reception one night after the show floor has closed. It is imperative that you keep your products and services at the forefront of the conversation while they are enjoying their snacks and drinks. Positioning your products throughout the venue and having numerous staff members available to answer questions and interact with guests is the best way to keep the message clear.

You will enjoy more success with your hospitality event if both your event and your trade show booth have a congruent presentation style. If you have a professional presenter making hourly presentations and product demonstrations in your booth during show hours, have them stick around for a couple hours after the close of the trade show so that they can do the same presentation at your hospitality event. This is a great way to reach those people that may have missed the presentation earlier in the day. If you have a magician at your booth, ask them to attend the hospitality event. A good magician can create a sense of belonging among sometimes-awkward attendees, and can set your company apart from others.

Keep in mind that hospitality events can be rather costly. Accordingly, you should consider if it is something that is likely to pay off for you down the road. In some industries, hospitality events appear to be quite standard. In others, however, they are not as common and may not be appreciated or well attended. Sit down with your trade show team and decide if a hospitality event fits into your budget and your show plans.

"The difference between the impossible and the possible lies in a person's determination."

– Tommy Lasorda, baseball manager

Chapter 13 – The Use of Magic

In 2000, Exhibitor Magazine published a survey showing that magical presentations are the #2 method for drawing and holding a crowd's attention at a tradeshow. In that same year, the Wall Street Journal reported that magic is the most effective way for companies to enjoy the greatest return on their often-limited trade show budget. As a professional magician and someone that has been in the trade show industry for dozens of years, I believe that a magician, used to his or her full potential, can wildly increase a company's trade show success. In this chapter, I will explain the imperative aspects of utilizing this well known method for garnering and retaining a trade show audience.

In the previous chapter, I discussed the importance of

having an effective presenter conduct live presentations and demonstrations in your company's booth. This is not only a sure way to draw a crowd to your booth, but can also be an effective tool for pre-qualifying prospects. There is no doubt that having a live presenter that will attract a healthy crowd and pare down that crowd during the presentation is a far better approach than attracting a huge unqualified mass of people by giving away a stuffed toy. If you make the mistake of trying to attract everyone, you will certainly find yourself with hundreds, if not thousands, of unqualified leads following the show. Because you have to sift through the whole host of unqualified leads, you will lose most of those that are qualified in the inevitable shuffle. It is much better to learn how to grab and hold the attention of only those attendees who are your company's best prospects. Therefore, it is worth it to take some time to learn about incorporating magic into your live presentation.

TRADE SHOW BUSINESS

As a professional entertainer and trade show presenter, I have learned what is effective and what is not in terms of putting on a show. This knowledge has become so engrained in me that it is now common sense. While it feels like common sense to me, I understand that in reality it is uncommon sense that has been cultivated through decades of experience. As you read on, you will learn my uncommon sense secrets to putting on a successful show. Uncommon sense is, in fact, little more than viewing things from an uncommon perspective.

Uncommon sense secret number one: The key to success in presenting information through a magician in a trade show setting is to format the presentation like a television show. You see, people love to be entertained. Entertainment, as we have learned through years of growing up watching sitcoms, comes at a very small but important price: commercials. We have all come to expect these small interruptions as part of the entertainment package. As we watch our favorite program, we know that we will be entertained for 10 or 15 minutes and then those colorful and sometimes entertaining commercials will flash across the screen in an effort to capture a modicum of our collective attention. Another 10 minutes of the show will be followed by more commercials. To be successful, broadcasters count on your willingness to watch those commercials, giving rise to sales for those companies smart enough to advertise through the medium of television. Often, people will learn about the newest and most up to date products through the marketing channel of advertising. This successful business model translates perfectly into trade show presentations resulting in more sales for your company. The crowd at a trade show is virtually starved for something entertaining. Consequently, they are quite willing to accept that quick commercial break between acts. As your prospects watch the woman being sawed in half or levitating, they almost certainly won't notice the direct selling technique underlying the presentation.

Uncommon sense secret number two: When designing your presentation, keep in mind that it is the "show" portion of your trade show experience that must be emphasized. Any presentation performed in your booth should be engaging and fun. Magic is the perfect medium for accomplishing this two-fold goal. Magic acts to grab the attention of passers by and hold that attention while your marketing message is memorably delivered. To best deliver this magical advertising message, your magician should incorporate no more than three key points. Each individual presentation should last no more than 10 to 15 minutes and should be delivered every hour on the hour. The shorter the presentations, the less time between shows is necessary. For instance, if your presentation is six minutes, you may be able to schedule repeat performances every 45 minutes. This is purely a matter of choice. The critical consideration is to be sure that your sales team has sufficient time to filter through the crowd collecting qualified leads before the next performance begins. In order to avoid repetition for those attendees that choose to return for a second look, you can plan two or three different shows and have them performed on a rotating basis. Choosing the right magician can enhance your ability to capture, qualify and entertain your target audience while interspersing your marketing message in a memorable way.

Uncommon sense secret number three: Just like major television networks, your marketing strategy must be carefully intertwined with the entertainment. Improperly timed commercials or commercials that overpower the entertainment will quickly diminish audience interest. In addition, when calculating what you should spend on hiring the right person to craft the perfect entertaining commercial, you should not skimp. Spending gads of money on the perfect display and the most quality brochures will help in making a good impression, but won't necessarily capture that perfect target audience and transform them into a paying customer. In contrast, investing in a quality performer has the potential to deliver more impact than all of your other marketing efforts combined. Accordingly, it pays to invest in this effective marketing tool.

THE OLDEST PROFESSION IN THE WORLD

While the phrase "the oldest profession in the world" conjures a particular line of work, I am convinced that magic, in fact, is the oldest profession in the world. There is a good reason why it is referred to as "turning a trick." In all seriousness, magic appeals to a universal audience and bridges language, cultural, and generational barriers. Nothing brings out natural human curiosity better than magic. As people watch a magic show, they are transported into a world full of possibilities. Adults suddenly regress and become childlike, even if just for a fleeting moment. Magic makes a person take a second and even third look in an effort to unravel the impossible image they have just witnessed. When used in marketing a product or service, magic is particularly effective because it makes people stop, look, listen and think. They tend to stop because they aren't sure of what it is they have just witnessed. They look intently to try to catch the trick that makes the impossible possible. They listen to every sound in an effort to catch any sound that might reveal the secret. And lastly, they think about what they are seeing and hearing because they are engaged in the mystery. Although most people are excited by the mystery of magic, some people feel foolish at being tricked, even if it is for the sake of entertainment. The style your performer adopts can go a long way to easing this small but important issue. You would be wise to take this issue into consideration when you are sitting down to plan the integration of your marketing presentation into your magic show. The goal of a marketing magician is not to fool the audience. Instead, the magician must strive to keep the presentation as fun-spirited and light hearted as possible. Magicians that try to be mysterious with powers the audience can never hope to capture tend to alienate rather than endear prospective clients. Since your goal is to capture, not repel, your audience, you should be careful to choose a performer that uses his or her tricks as a gimmick to show how your product or service works just like magic!

HIRE A PROFESSIONAL MAGICIAN

Once you have decided to hire a magician to perform in your booth, make certain that you hire a true professional. Most magicians listed in the yellow pages are accustomed to performing at country fairs and kids' birthday parties. Although these types of magicians are quite skilled at performing tricks, they rarely are skilled at interweaving a marketing message into their performance in an effective way. What you need to look for is someone who has specific experience in trade show magic. Don't rely on demo tapes – they may be fun to watch, but even the average backyard magician is capable of editing an impressive demo tape that doesn't show a fair picture of his or her capabilities. Insist on a live meeting where you and your team can properly evaluate the magician's skills and personality. Remember, your magician will stand out from the crowd and be recognized throughout the show floor so you want him or her to project the professional image befitting of your company.

Also, be sure to discuss exactly what type of magic tricks your magician will be performing for your audience. This is an area where bigger is, indeed, better. Larger illusions can offer greater impact. I have found it works extremely well because people are accustomed to seeing these illusions on TV or large stages at great distances. But, when an attendee can see one of these large illusions up close they are even more amazed and curious. Let's put it this way, everybody has seen a card trick or has an uncle that can do them. How many have seen a person sawed in half or levitated above their heads up close? This is something they can rave about and they will. Most people who have attended trade shows have happened by a magician standing at a podium having the audience pick a card or make a dollar bill vanish. Not because it's a great spectacle, but because magicians love tricks that "pack small and play big." That is not necessarily the type of show you want to put on for your prospects. What you want to create is a real show, something that everyone in the crowd will be able to see, and something that will leave a lasting impression long after they have moved along the trade show floor. Large-scale tricks that often involve members of the audience are the best way to go.

MAGICIAN'S DRESS CODE

If you have been to a trade show and seen the small card toting magician, you may or may not have noticed that he or she was dressed in a sport coat and slacks. This type of dress blends right in with the rest of the booth staff. Some magicians even sport the company polo shirt in an effort to put on that unified front I discussed in chapter 10. I am absolutely convinced that this is the wrong way to go. The reason is simple; when a magician blends in with your staff, he or she is perceived as a staff member. However, when a prospect approaches with a specific question about your product and the magician is unable to give the in-depth answer that your team members would be able to give, the overall image of your company is tarnished. Since the role of the magician is to stand out and entertain people, the chosen attire should be entertaining as well. Upscale attire with a splash of color or sparkle will set the magician apart, not only from the rest of your staff, but from the rest of the attendees and exhibitors as well.

TIPS FOR MAGIC SUCCESS

Although there are professional magicians willing to do the work, your company does not have to hire a magician to put on a magic show. Yes, a member of your staff can execute an effective magic show so long as they have the right personality. As a thank you for reading this book, I would like to extend an invitation for you to review Milligan's Marketing Magic program. See the bonus section of this book for more information. I have specifically developed this self-working magic program to allow companies to turn any friendly sales representative into a marketing magician capable of doing tricks that will impress virtually any audience. Take the next step, and find out how **Milligan's Marketing Magic** can help you increase sales at your next trade show and beyond. Just complete the fax request form in the Bonus Section at the back of this book for a **FREE Report** on how to use these specific marketing tools to build your business. Whether you are looking for advice on improving your trade show marketing copy, using marketing to attract more business, or improving other aspects of your trade show experience, help is just a fax or phone call away. This report is at no cost or obligation to you. Once you see what the full program can offer, you will be able to make a decision regarding the implementation of this and other programs, such as the Magical Icebreakers, that I have to offer. You see, magic marketing will work for any business. I have presented programs for everything from hi-tech industries, mom and pop shops, to mortuaries. Yes, they do trade shows, too. Business is business and marketing is marketing, no matter the business.

Consider taking a short cut to trade show success by having an expert create your presentation for you, from beginning to end. Since it is sometimes difficult for a company to look inward and know exactly what to do, you may choose to hire someone who can help you implement your trade show marketing strategy. What if that person can drastically improve your presentation and write your marketing copy? What if they can train your top sales representative to become your company's in-house trade show magician and key presenter? What if this resulted in dozens of qualified prospects being attracted to your booth for all the right reasons? That is exactly what I am offering. I urge you to invest in my expertise and experience; an investment that I guarantee will pay for itself many times over.

SUCCESS STORY

Many years ago, I created one of my first custom trade show presentations for a client that included a *full marketing program* to complement our magic show. The project was for a small residential/business alarm company called Alert Security. According to their goals, they chose to have a standard 10′ x 10′ booth at the show. We used a three-prong attack by pre-show promoting the event with post card announcements to past clients and past show attendees. Next, we created incentives to visit our client's booth where we presented a fun magic show that highlighted our client's product. In conclusion, we made sure that the follow-up after the show was direct, focused and consistent. Our client was shocked to see the crowds of people that were attracted to their booth as a result of both the marketing efforts and the magic. But, the real shocker came at the close of the show; our client collected 379% more qualified leads than they were able to in the previous year. And, within just 60 days, they did 210% more business than they had after the previous year's show. This was certainly no accident. Instead, it was the predictable result of a carefully planned, customized marketing program. Pre-show marketing, post-show follow up, and effective presentations – these are all steps that lead to stellar results. The trick is to incorporate all three parts into a comprehensive program that will ensure that no good prospect falls through the cracks. This is my expertise, my passion, and my offer to you.

"Confidence…thrives on honesty, on honor, on the sacredness of obligations, on faithful protection and on unselfish performance. Without them it cannot live."

– Franklin Delano Roosevelt, 32nd US president

Chapter 14 – Exhibiting Logistics

As a company makes the decision to exhibit its products and services at a trade show, the company's trade show team will undoubtedly find itself faced with many logistical questions and issues that have to be addressed before the show starts. Your team will need to have the full support of your company's management in order to address those questions in a timely way with confidence. To encounter the least problems, your team should begin preparing the logistics of your show weeks, indeed, months in advance. Doing so will benefit your team in myriad ways, including both cost and time savings.

CHOOSING A LOCATION

Although it is arguable whether the location of your booth on the trade show floor has any real impact on the level of success your company experiences in exhibiting, it is nonetheless worth considering with a great degree of care. The Center for Exhibition Industry Research conducted a study in which it was shown that 23 percent of attendees consider the location of a booth when deciding to visit it or not.[2] Of course, this research strongly suggests that the decision of where to locate an exhibit on a trade show floor is comparable to the decision of where to locate a business on a city street. The better the location, the more likely patrons will be exposed to your business, which certainly leads to more sales. Since every venue and every exhibit hall is different, I suggest you consider the following questions when picking a spot:

Do you want to be near the entrances or exits?

Since the entrance is usually a high traffic area, you may want to try and grab a booth space there. You can then capture the attendees as they walk fresh and eager into the exhibit hall. On the other hand, if there are walkways that are designated for exit only, you will probably not be able to attract passersby since they will be ready to leave the show by the time they make it to your booth.

---

2   July 1982 "Trade Show Bureau Research Report #13."

Are there restrictions on display height in certain parts of the hall?

To avoid potential problems, your display should be as universally accommodating as possible. However, if you have any doubt about the height allowance, make sure to check with the show management. You definitely don't want to be stuck near obstructing columns, low ceilings, large overhead beams, dark areas, or dead-end aisles.

Do you want to be near the restrooms/ meeting rooms/restaurants?

Being located near a restroom will definitely draw traffic to the area at all times throughout the show, but this won't necessarily draw traffic to your booth. Restaurants also attract a constant flow of people, but usually that crowd is taking a break and will not delay their break just because your booth is nearby. Plus, if you're too close, your booth could become a dumping ground for paper plates and cups.

Where will the size of your display be best accommodated?

If you have a large display, you will probably want to select a large island or peninsula spot. A smaller display can be just as effective along the outskirts of the hall or in one of the rows.

Do you want to be near or far from the competition?

Sometimes, being close to the competition is not always a bad thing. If you position your booth near an industry leader who attracts throngs of quality attendees, you may reap the benefits of the leader's marketing, since some of those attendees are sure to stop by your booth as well.

Do you want to be in a corner?

As a rule of thumb, you should avoid the back corners of the exhibit hall. The front corners sometimes draw a lot of traffic, but this may be risky as well. It is best to be in the middle or at the end of a row where traffic will constantly and naturally flow past your booth.

Do you want to be near a window?

You may want the added benefit of a great view from your booth, but keep in mind that sunlight could get in the way during certain times of the day. It could cause your staff to become overheated and could shine too much sunlight on your display, causing a glare.

You should be careful to thoroughly examine the floor plan before you sign your company up for a booth space. Most shows have this information available online. If this information is not readily available, then you can ask the show management to furnish the floor plan to you. You want to be sure you are getting a complete picture before committing your company to the expense of exhibiting in a show. It is also very helpful if the show plan includes the names and booth locations of those exhibitors who have already committed to exhibit in the show.

KNOW THE SHOW RULES

Just as soon as you and your team determine that your company will be an exhibitor at a certain trade show, I suggest you act without delay. Taking action immediately will give you a number of advantages you wouldn't otherwise enjoy. For example, the earlier you commit to exhibiting in the show, the better chance you will have of landing the perfect location. The first thing to do is to obtain a copy of the exhibitor manual from the show management team. Don't make the mistake of assuming that exhibitor manuals are not worth spending the time reading over. Read each section of it in detail, making sure to look out for any tidbit of information that may be of value to your company.

Since each show management team, exhibit hall and show as a whole are distinct one from another, you can expect that each exhibitor manual will be equally as distinct as the shows themselves. Here are a few things to look for when reading the exhibitor manual:

- Show location
- Show days and hours
- Designated setup and breakdown days and hours
- Exhibitor booth layout
- Deadlines for ordering exhibit space
- Exhibit space application
- Deadlines to order power, labor, Internet, etc.

- Deadlines to order exhibitor badges
- Order forms for various services
- Hotel recommendations
- Program listing requirements
- Rules of the show
- Liability insurance requirements

As you read through the manual, make detailed notes for yourself regarding what will have to be done and when. Use a calendar to plan out a show preparation timeline and specifically assign each task to a reliable team member. You will benefit in many ways if you stick to your schedule and meet your self-imposed deadlines. Since most shows offer a discount for ordering booth space and other services early, being organized and thorough is a sure way to save money and make sure you are prepared for the show in advance.

EXHIBIT INSURANCE

Since your company's exhibit probably cost your company a pretty penny and is intended to travel to various shows throughout the years, an exhibit insurance policy should definitely be in the show budget. While some general contractors present at the show will provide exhibitors with insurance, this is the exception rather than the rule. In fact, there is often a waiver printed in the finest of type in your exhibitor services manual that limits liability to a nominal amount of $100 per lost or damaged item. Needless to say, this modicum of coverage falls far below the cost of even a modest exhibit.

In order to have comprehensive coverage that will genuinely give you peace of mind, you should include your company as a rider on your existing corporate insurance policy. If that isn't feasible for whatever reason, you can buy insurance through the transportation company you have contracted with to transport your display to and from the show location. Buying insurance from the carrier is usually more expensive, but it can be quick and easy. I have, however, found that it is hard to collect on a claim from the transportation company if need be, so the best way to protect your investment is by adding your exhibit onto your general insurance policy and make sure it is covered during transit too.

EXHIBIT RESTRICTIONS

As your team plans for the show, you should determine well in advance whether your exhibit will meet the requirements of the trade show management. If your company already has an exhibit, you must be sure that its dimensions are acceptable for the show you are considering. If the display is too large or otherwise doesn't meet the show requirements, you will need to consider an alternate exhibit strategy such as purchasing another display or renting a display that does meet the show's restrictions. Whether you are planning to use an existing display or purchase a new display, you will need to ascertain the show's exhibit restrictions to properly plan. The exhibitor manual you obtain from show management will list the following dimensions of both the show floor as well as the restrictions on the display itself. The most common dimensions and restrictions include the following:

- Ceiling height

- Dock door width and height

- Maximum display height

- Maximum display width

- Lighting restrictions

SHIPPING THE EXHIBIT

There are a couple different options when it comes to shipping the exhibit to the venue. Your shipping decision will ultimately be dictated by the size of your exhibit.

Common Carriers

If your exhibit is a portable system designed for a 10x10 or 10x20 booth space, it will most likely be within the size limitations of such common carriers as UPS and DHL. You can arrange for pickup at your location or you may be able to drop the crate off at their facilities. I suggest spending the extra money on overnight shipping versus ground shipping; the less time the exhibit spends in transport, the less wear and tear it will incur.

Freight Carriers

An exhibit that does not fit the weight requirements of these common carriers will have to be shipped via freight. There are literally dozens of different freight carriers, so it is very important to choose one that will treat your exhibit with care. Adcom Worldwide and ELITeXPO Cargo Systems are two companies that specialize in transporting exhibits. These are companies I have used and have full confidence in their doing the job right. You will find their contact information at the end of this section and in my resources guide. The difference between using a carrier who is a specialist in transporting tradeshow exhibits versus a carrier that is not, is that using a company with particular knowledge of the issues particular to trade shows can save your company a bundle of money. One area that a carrier specializing in exhibits can address is the inevitable line of shipments arriving at the show all in unison. This common problem encountered with delivery of exhibits to the show floor is the long wait time for the driver before he or she can get a bay to deliver your exhibit. General type carriers will often charge extra for this wait time while specialist carriers often do not. In fact, they really just build this extra cost into the price but usually at a reduced rate.

Adcom Worldwide, Inc
877-700-2700
www.adcomworldwide.com

ELITeXPO Cargo Systems
800-543-5484 x3821
www.elitexpo.com

Ship Early

No matter the size of your display or by which shipping method it is delivered to the show location, I encourage you to ship the display days, if not weeks, before the start of the show. The reason is simple. Exhibitors usually have a small window of opportunity in the days before the show to get their exhibit in the door and get it set up on time. If you have missed the deadline for whatever reason, the loading docks close and you are no longer allowed to bring your display in. By shipping ahead of time, you can easily avoid this unpleasant situation. You will pay a bit extra for drayage or storage at the show location, but it is well worth the money to make sure that you will have your display when and where you need it.

LABOR AT THE SHOW

Once a display arrives at the show, you have to consider the logistics of having it set up. The exhibitor manual will indicate whether the trade show is a union or non-union show. Whether the show is a union show or not dictates whether you will be permitted to choose who will set up your exhibit. Non-union shows permit exhibitors to elect any of the following choices with respect to set up: they can use their own staff, the laborers provided by the show management team, or an outside contractor. On the contrary, if it is a union show, as most are, exhibitors are required to hire the show's union contractors to transport the displays onto the show floor, set them up and dismantle them at the conclusion of the show.

Union Rules

The rule that exhibitors must use union staff for all labor, including set up and dismantling, is limited as follows; if an exhibitor can carry the display in and is able to set it up in under ½ hour, they are not required to pay for labor. Of course, if the exhibit is large and must to be transported to the booth, then the exhibitor will be required to use the show's union labor. Even though you cannot control who will be setting up and dismantling your exhibit, you can control how it will be done.

The first means of taking control of the labor in your booth is to assume the task of supervising the laborers yourself. You must, of course, know all the ins and outs of assembling, dismantling, and re-packing your exhibit, but familiarizing yourself with your display is well worth the effort you will expend. Laborers at trade shows obviously have a great deal of experience assembling and dismantling exhibits, but that does not necessarily translate into how to assemble your particular exhibit. Supervising the union team will result in a number of benefits for you. First, you will be able to carefully direct the laborers, minimizing damage to your exhibit. Second, you will cut down on the cost of labor because you won't need to hire a supervisor to guide the work. Third, set up time will be reduced because you will be able direct the laborers on the specifics of how your exhibit goes together and dismantles.

Romancing the Union

Most people would agree that they would rather work with a friendly team of people who honestly put in a good day's work than with a bunch of grumpy employees who stop working the instant our backs are turned. The same concept is true at a trade show. Even though you may be frustrated at the fact that the show management is has forced you to use their laborers and you may find it a hassle to work with people you don't know, you should nonetheless give your best effort to making the experience friendly rather than tense.

Start out by personally introducing yourself to the exhibitor services contact as soon as you arrive at the show location. Ask them the best means of contacting them so you can be in touch right away if necessary. By making this introduction and obtaining contact information, you will have ready access to their assistance if you experience any problems during the set up or dismantle of your exhibit.

Even more important than establishing a connection with the exhibit services contact is setting the stage for a good working relationship with the union laborers. These are hardworking people are there for the sole purpose of getting your booth ready for the show. If you start off with a friendly approach and make them feel they are an important component of your company's success at the show, you will find they are more eager to do a good job in a timely manner. You can start this relationship off on the right foot by introducing yourself warmly, bringing your team coffee, and making sure they understand that you are interested in a team approach. By making this small initial effort, you will smooth the progress for all your labor needs.

DOCUMENT YOUR EXHIBIT

Once you and your team have set up the exhibit in preparation for the show, I suggest taking detailed digital pictures of the final product. Make sure to get all angles of the display from close up to far away. This serves two important purposes. First, it provides a clear image of what the display should look like when it has been correctly installed, which can serve as a model for your company should they need to set up the exhibit in your absence. Second, having detailed pictures of the display allows you to inspect any damage or any wear and tear that might have occurred during shipment or setup. By knowing where the damage is, you can resolve the problem before the next show.

CHECKLIST EVERYTHING

Checklists are the only way to assure that you have assembled all the show essentials in preparation for show day. It is critical to have all necessary show items with you when arriving at the show. As your team packs their personal and business belongings, you can use the handy checklist provided on the next page to make sure you have all the essentials needed for a successful show.

Business Needs	Booth Needs
☐ Business Cards	☐ Extension Cord
☐ Literature/Brochures	☐ Paper towels / Swiffer
☐ Premiums	☐ Stapler / Tape / Scissors
☐ Product Samples	☐ Self-Adhesive Velcro
☐ Computers	☐ Permanent Markers
☐ Lead Sheets	☐ Tool Kit
☐ Pens	☐ Trash Bags
☐ Exhibit	☐ Display Instructions
☐ Exhibitor Manual	☐ Shipping Labels
Personal Needs	**Travel Needs**
☐ Comfortable Shoes	☐ GPS/Maps/Directions
☐ Pain Medicine	☐ Travel Tickets
☐ Hand Sanitizer	☐ Hotel Information
☐ Breath Mints	☐ Required Clothing
☐ Water	☐ Cash/Credit Cards
☐ Snacks	☐ Locations of Nearby Restaurants
☐ Small First-aid Kit	☐ Locations of Office Supply Stores
☐ Safety Pins	☐ Receipts for Services
☐ Sewing Kit	☐ Toiletries

POST-SHOW SHIPPING

Organization and thinking ahead doesn't conclude with the show. As the show closes and your team prepares to break down your booth and head home, I would like to draw your attention to a few shipping pointers.

All components of the display should be packed up in order and checked off on a thorough checklist to ensure that no parts are missing or damaged. If you identify a problem with the display, then it can be addressed upon your return to the office. If it is necessary to fix any part of your display, you should do so immediately. If you delay fixing damaged parts of your exhibit, you may forget entirely and be unprepared when your next show date arrives.

One of my clients puts fabric softener sheets into her company's display cases. This ensures that the display will stay fresh and help beat that musty odor after several weeks or months of storage.

Also, you should be sure that the display cases you are using for transport are the right fit for your display and your graphics. Forcing pieces of your display into a case that is too small will result in damage to the unit. It also complicates the post-show packing process as the show laborers will likely be short on patience by that point and won't have the time to use sufficient care in repacking your system. Likewise, you don't want a case that is too big as your exhibit pieces will then slosh around during shipping, which will certainly result in damage. A great idea for shipping is using collapsible plastic crates. They are generally durable and take up very little space when not in use.

DISPLAY MANAGEMENT

Without question, the storage, transportation, set-up, and breakdown of an exhibit are difficult tasks. Smoothly accomplishing these tasks in a timely fashion requires the coordination and valuable time of some of your company's key employees. Because specialists in the trade show industry understand how this use of company resources impedes the work of the company, they have started offering to outsource many of these tasks.

Most exhibit design companies offer this popular service. Basically, once a company of your choosing manufactures your display, you can then choose to have that company handle the logistics surrounding the use of your display.

Management and storage companies can perform all or some of the following tasks:

- <u>Store your display at their storage facility</u>
  – Be aware that you may have to show proof of insurance for your display, even when it's stored at another location.

- <u>Ship the display to and from each show location</u>
  – The exhibit house can handle all of the details of getting your display to where it needs to be on time.

- <u>Supervise the set-up and breakdown of your display at each show</u> – The exhibit house can provide a designated person whose only job for that time period is to supervise the set up of your display before the show and the take down immediately following the show.

- <u>Check over the condition of your display</u> – Following the closing of each show, as the display arrives back at their storage facility, the exhibit house can do a thorough check of the condition of your display. If any parts need to be fixed or replaced, they can handle that aspect as well.

Using professional display management services can be beneficial to your organization. If you choose to utilize some or all of these available services, your time before, during, and after the show should be virtually headache-free. Of course, the biggest benefit in using such services is that you and your team will have a lot more time to concentrate on pre-show marketing, live presentations, and post-show follow-ups without having to worry about the mundane logistics of exhibiting.

"The road to success is always under construction."

-Lily Tomlin, actress

Chapter 15 – After The Show Ends

As alluded to in earlier chapters, the post-show efforts of your team are certainly as important, if not more important, than your pre-show efforts. Too often, I have seen a company's sales staff leaving the show looking tired and clearly assuming their work is done. On the contrary, the conclusion of the show is really the beginning of the work for your sales team.

POST-SHOW SURVEYS

Create a Survey

I suggest creating a short survey to help conduct your post-show market research. Your survey should touch on the effectiveness of your booth presentation, why attendees chose to stop by your booth, and a few other questions that might interest you following the show. The results of such a survey can be invaluable to your organization and can ensure that your team does an even better job of exhibiting at the next trade show.

Survey Format

To be most effective, the survey should be short and to the point, and should be no longer than the front of one page. You can choose to conduct the survey in e-mail format, so that your attendees can easily answer the questions with just a few clicks of a mouse. You can also decide to mail out the survey, making sure to include a postage-paid return envelope for your attendees to use. No matter which method you choose to use for survey distribution, I strongly suggest you offer an incentive for its completion and submission. Whether it is something small like a calendar magnet with your company logo, or a monetary incentive in the form of a discount on the next purchase from your company, an incentive will increase the likelihood that the surveys will be returned.

Outsource It

If you find yourself and your team too busy to conduct and track the results of your market research efforts after the trade show, you can choose to outsource this function. Don't bother contacting a high-end market research organization for this task. Instead, you are better off contacting the business-marketing department at your local college or university. The school is a rich source of students who will be more than willing to take on this task for you as an educational experience. The student can design the survey questions, distribute the survey to the appropriate contacts, and collect and analyze the results.

Generally, students will undertake these assignments with vigor. The standard cost of this type of research is very small when conducted in an educational setting. Sometimes there is no fee, as the assignment can fulfill a student's unpaid internship requirement. Since it may take some time to find this student and give them enough information to work with, I suggest locating such a student before the trade show starts, so that they will be ready to execute your plan immediately following the show.

BUDGET COMPARISON

If your company is like most exhibiting companies including both veterans and newcomers, you will likely have overspent your pre-set trade show budget. To get a clear picture of where each exhibiting dollar went, you should take the time to compare your planned budget to your actual spending.

Remember the budget that your team had set when you first started planning for the trade show a few months ago? You should compare that proposed budget to the actual dollar amount spent within each category. Let me remind you of the seven basic spending categories likely included in your original budget:

Expenditure	Planned	Actual
Exhibit Purchase or Rental		
Booth Space Rental		
Pre-Show Marketing		
Live Talent or Attraction		
Show Staff and Training		
Show Services (power, etc.)		
Hot Lead Follow-ups		
Post-Show Marketing		

Start out by taking all of your receipts and separating them by category. You can then easily add up what you have spent on each general item and compare your original figures to your actual figures. This will identify the areas where you have overspent, under spent or hit your planned spending limit. If you then break each category down even further into a detailed list of expenditures, you will begin to understand how to avoid this discrepancy at future trade shows.

Was your transportation to the show more expensive than anticipated? By planning far in advance, you may be able to take advantage of flight discounts and specials next time. Was the design and manufacturing of your exhibit more expensive than anticipated? Consider using a different design approach next time it is needed; but, if you have invested in a quality exhibit, console yourself with the fact that a new exhibit won't be needed for years to come. Did shipping your exhibit and supplies to the show become more expensive than anticipated? Find out what you can do next time to cut down on this cost.

Once you know exactly where you have overspent, it will be easier to plan a more realistic budget for the next trade show.

MANAGING LEADS

In my experience, I have found that the single most important task you and your team will undertake following the conclusion of a trade show is how you will manage the leads that were so painstakingly collected during the course of the show. The leads left by the trashcan will result in wasted time and money as well as poor results from the long hours invested. It is vital, as discussed earlier, to have a set plan for how the leads will be handled. It is not enough to run a smooth show, talk to many promising prospects, and ensure that your lead manager takes the box of leads back to the office. Instead, you must plan a strategy to follow up on all of those leads as soon as possible. Prospects are not likely to remember to call you, but they will probably gladly take a call from you, especially if they expect one.

Consistency is Key

All of the leads should be distributed to those salespeople who will be responsible for the follow up. Your sales people will likely welcome this task, as it is far superior to the list of cold calls sitting on their desks. In addition, if they themselves were part of the trade show sales team, they will have a personal contact with those prospects that will likely result in a sale. Whenever possible, you should make an effort to distribute the leads in such a way as to provide continuity for both the salesperson and the prospect. By this I mean that those people with whom Jane interacted with at the show should get a follow-up call from Jane herself rather than some other member of your sales team. Your lead form should clearly indicate what the prospect is expecting as the next step and with whom they interacted at the show. If Jane promised to call the prospect for an in-depth discussion of the benefits of your product or service, then she should make that valuable call as soon as is practicable. If, on the other hand, she promised to send them literature, she should send it out immediately and then follow up with a phone call.

It is important that your next contact with the prospect following the show is one that the prospect expects and that this contact occurs within just days following the closing of the show. To make an even nicer impression on your clients and prospects, you can send a personalized, hand-written thank you card. If you feel that your staff is too busy for this time-consuming task, it can easily be outsourced to an eager intern or student.

Five Star Follow-Up

I suggest doing a Five Star Follow-Up with all viable prospects. A Five Star Follow-Up consists of at least five points of contact between your sales person and each qualified prospect after the show. Whether the first contact is via mail or phone, each subsequent contact should be at a predetermined interval and should be expected and welcomed by the prospect. You can contact them on a weekly or monthly basis. Certainly, by the fifth contact with the prospect, it will become apparent if the prospect will become your company's client or not.

Track Your Efforts

The follow-up efforts of your staff should be closely tracked in a central system using pre-determined timelines. Whether you use spreadsheets, a computer program, or another medium, it is important that each staffer understands the importance of tracking leads. Some warm prospects will inevitably grow cold, while some prospects may buy from you immediately or a few months down the line. You should carefully record the results of each interaction with a prospect so that at a later date those results can be closely analyzed.

EVALUATING YOUR SUCCESS

As the trade show wraps up, you may be wondering, "How did we do?" Over the years, I have been able to distill the two major mistakes companies make when evaluating the success of their trade show effort. First, exhibitors fail to even examine the success or lack thereof. Because examining one's success takes conscious effort, people will simply jump back into the daily grind without determining whether the event was a success or not. In my opinion, this is a grave mistake. Without proper evaluation, a company just doesn't know if the show was worth it, if anything went wrong, and if it makes financial sense to exhibit again.

The second mistake is to equate a company's measure of exhibiting success with the number of leads collected. Companies mistakenly assume that the more leads they collected, the more successful the show was overall. Although a company with a good exhibiting strategy has tried to qualify leads before collecting them, simply looking at the volume of leads doesn't mean success. It is much wiser to look at your Return on Investment when looking at how successful the show was.

Return on Investment

Properly evaluating your financial success following a trade show is crucial. Your Return on Investment is essentially a comparison of show results to show goals. If one of your show objectives was to make direct sales at the show, you should start out by calculating your show revenue immediately upon your return to the office. Most likely, you won't recoup your trade show costs with sales closed directly on the trade show floor. However, by conducting a close evaluation of your post-show lead tracking system, you should be able to determine which leads turned into customers, calculate how much revenue was generated from each new customer, and project how many other leads are likely to turn into new customers in the near future.

This Return on Investment evaluation should be conducted at intervals of 60, 90, 180, and 300 days after the close of the show. You may want to adjust this time frame to your company's sales cycle to better reflect the appropriate amount of time it would take for a typical customer to make a purchasing decision for your product or service. Only then will you be able to see how much of your trade show costs you have recouped.

Objectives

If you are like most companies, financial gain is probably at the top of your list of trade show goals. Setting this fact aside for a moment, there is no doubt that your company's success at a trade show is not only measured in monetary terms. Looking back on the show goals that you had written down in the beginning, it is important to completely understand if all of your goals have been met. To better help you with this task, here are some questions to ask yourself and your show staff:

- How many presentations were done in your booth?

- How many pre-scheduled appointments showed?

- Was there adequate staffing for the booth?

- Was the staff adequately trained?

- Was lead management handled effectively?

- Did the booth space accommodate your needs?

- Did the exhibit delivery and setup run smoothly?

- Were there things that your staff wasn't prepared for?

Asking yourself questions such as these will give you insight into what went wrong and what went right at the show. By thoroughly understanding the mistakes made, the things that worked, and by really listening to your sales people's comments, you will be given a real chance to do a better job at your company's next trade show.

Deciding to return

As most trade shows run on an annual basis, your company will have just a few months following the close of the show to decide if you want to exhibit at the same show again. If you are on top of your numbers and know where you stand, you'll want to make the decision to come back before the last day of your current show. Most shows offer substantial savings if you rebook on the spot for next year's show. To make the right decision that will positively impact your bottom line, you should be gathering the honest opinions from several different sources from day one of the show. Ask your staff and your outside vendors if they feel this particular show is working well for your company. If your vendors and suppliers, as well as your competition, are present at the show, they often have different insights into the effectiveness of the show. Also, consider surveying some of your customers and your best prospects if they will continue attending the show in the future and if they think that it is a good place for your company to have a presence. They'll be honest with you if you let them know that you are just gathering information. By understanding the pluses and minuses of the specific show that you are interested in revisiting, you will be sure to make an educated decision on your future investment in the show.

"Kindness is a language that the deaf can hear and the blind can read."

— *Mark Twain, author*

Chapter 16 – A Trade Show Veteran's Cost-Cutting Strategies

In this chapter, I will focus on some cost-cutting ideas that exhibitors can implement into their trade show plan to start saving money even before the show begins. With a bit of creativity, it is possible to convey a professional image to your customers without having to pay professional prices. Over the many years that I have been in this business, I have accumulated the following list of tips and tricks that will get you well on your way to successful exhibiting with a lower cash outlay.

If you are like most trade show exhibitors, your company probably has less than 50 employees. No matter the size of your company, it is likely that you want to exhibit on a budget.

Your goal is certainly to look professional and experienced, but to do so on as meager a budget as possible. The following are twenty cost-cutting strategies you can implement.

1. <u>Bigger isn't always better</u> – As you are evaluating the different shows available, remember that bigger is not always better. Depending on the show's location, clientele, and other factors, a smaller regional show may be just as effective in meeting your exhibiting goals as a larger show. Considering that you will usually pay much less for booth space at a smaller show, this could be a good cost-cutting strategy. If you conduct proper pre-show marketing, a smaller show can be just as effective as a larger one.

2. <u>Rent your exhibit</u> – If you are thinking about exhibiting at your first trade show, or if your company doesn't plan on regularly exhibiting, it may be wise to rent an exhibit as opposed to buying one. This cuts your costs significantly, while still making you look professional and polished. This is also a great way to try out an exhibit to see if you like the way its configuration works for you. If you decide to buy the exhibit later on, many trade show companies will apply the rental cost to the purchase price.

3. <u>Alternative shipping</u> – If you use a drayage service for your display and materials, the price can add up quickly. To cut down on this cost, consider having the items shipped to your hotel and then transporting them to the show yourself. This will require a bit more work on your

part, but will save you a fair amount of money. Of course, this only makes sense if your containers are small enough to be easily handled by one or two people.

4. <u>Outsource to students</u> – Make a list of all of the services you will need for the upcoming show. Most of those things can be outsourced in a way that conserves your budget dollars. Consider using freelance professionals or students who can provide graphic design, marketing, survey taking, and other services for you at a fraction of the cost.

5. <u>Trade services with local schools</u> – Contact your local high school or college in order to find interested students who are willing to perform work for you for a modest wage. Depending on your industry and your expertise, you may even be able to barter your services to the school in exchange for students' work. Offer to speak on the subject or donate some of your time or services to the school. Such tasks as printing, graphic arts, and videotaping can have a perfectly professional a look when performed by students.

6. <u>Use what you have</u> – Consider transporting all of your own equipment to each trade show. This includes tables, chairs, flat screen monitors, laptops, etc. It is better to ship these items and set them up yourself than to pay for rent and delivery each time. If you decide to save money by shipping your own equipment, make sure not to skimp on the shipping containers. This is particularly true with frag-

ile items such as computers and monitors. You don't want to have to run out and purchase new equipment once you see that yours has arrived at the show damaged.

7.   <u>Check out various flying options</u> – If the trade show you have chosen is a plane flight away, consider how you can save money on airline tickets for your staff. Start checking ticket prices months before the show. Also, consider whether your team can fly into a nearby city and rent a car to drive to the show location. Many times, adjacent, small town airports offer discounts that the larger ones don't.

8.   <u>Consider using false deadlines</u> – As you write down your trade show plan and share it with your team in the months or weeks prior to the show's start, consider setting deadlines for the completion of various tasks a week earlier than they are actually due. Even if a team member happens to miss the deadline by a couple of days, you will still ensure that all of the items are ordered, printed, shipped, etc. before the real deadline. This will avoid those costly late charges that can ruin your carefully planned budget.

9.   <u>Schedule labor at the show very carefully</u> – Since overtime charges can be very expensive, make sure to allow ample time during normal working hours for the setup of your exhibit. Overtime charges usually apply in the evening and on weekends, so it is best to set up your exhibit during the week if possible.

10. <u>Don't waste paper and money</u> – Since you have learned that it is a waste to give away expensive brochures and binders to the attendees at the show, consider leaving them behind and giving out a simple one-page summary of your products or services. This cuts down on the cost of shipping bulky brochures and binders to the show.

11. <u>Plan ahead</u> – Plan for each trade show at least six months in advance. Most trade show management companies offer discounts for early birds and impose penalties on latecomers. Being an early bird permits you to take advantage of every discount that is made available. Also, by planning ahead and having enough time to consider all of the details, you are sure to have a smooth trade show experience.

12. <u>Take advantage of all discounts</u> – When you communicate with the shipping company or other service provider, make sure to tell them if you plan on using their services again in the future. Many times, they will be able to offer you a discount if you are going to be a repeat customer or if you have used their services in the past.

13. <u>Exhibit with others</u> – If your company is a retailer or distributor for a larger manufacturer, consider the possibility of exhibiting with your manufacturer. Many times, large manufacturers will happily invite quality salespeople to staff their booth. This cuts down on their staffing costs and gives your company the chance to exhibit at a fraction of the price. If you do consider this option, clarify

with your manufacturer exactly what the ground rules will be for the show. You want to know exactly what your responsibilities will be and how the resulting leads will be handled.

14. <u>Invite others to exhibit with you</u> – If suppliers and independent representatives are affiliated with your company, you can find out if they would be interested in sponsoring a part of your exhibit. For a fee, you can allow them to be present in your booth and to represent your product. This requires careful planning and training on your part but can be a great cost-cutting tool. Just make sure that the people you invite into your booth have the ability and willingness to represent your company in the proper light.

15. <u>Use the smallest exhibit possible</u> – Depending on the show venue and on your exhibiting goals, you may be able to get away with using an inexpensive tabletop display along with an imprinted table cover. As long as you still follow the principles of effective exhibit design, a tabletop display may cut down on your exhibiting budget tremendously while giving you the same overall results. If you do choose to use a smaller display, you will have the results you want if you assure that your marketing message is being clearly delivered to the show attendees.

16. <u>Fill your booth with banners</u> – Since banners can be easily rolled up into a lightweight, portable package, they

are a great way to save money on shipping. Banners can take the place of bulky display panels that are heavier and larger to ship. Banner stands come in a variety of styles from static stands to automatic, retractable stands. They can be printed in color and can be single or double sided. Just remember the tips on printing graphics from Chapter 9 and make sure to convey your marketing message whether you decide to use banners or not.

17. <u>Create a Starbucks® effect</u> – If your show budget and goals allow for a large display, consider breaking up this display into several smaller ones located throughout the trade show floor. Make each booth look and feel exactly the same and you will create a feeling of continuity among the attendees. Your exhibiting dollar will go further by allowing your salespeople to reach more prospects than they would with just one location.

18. <u>Utilize your magician as much as possible</u> – If you have a magician or other performer conducting presentations in your booth, utilize every minute of their time by keeping them busy between presentations. This does not mean have a non-stop presentation in your booth, but take advantage of their marketing power outside the booth. A magician can walk the show floor and do street-type magic in the aisles, in the food court, and in other public places. Most other acts or presenters cannot get away with this type of promotion, but just about everyone loves good magic. If your other timed in-booth presentations

are promoted in this way, you'll get a giant jump on your competition and chances are they will not even catch on that you are marketing outside your booth. This is a fantastic way to get your message to those who might have missed your booth. Allow your magician to constantly be promoting your company and inviting attendees to the show that just happens to be in your booth. Now, it is important this is done as a soft sell and not a blatant advertisement for your company. It should just be fun and an invitation to see more.

19. Cannibalize your old display – If you have exhibited many times in the past and your display now needs to be refreshed, don't assume that you have to purchase a whole new display. Many times, unless your display has been badly damaged in a fire or an accident, you can salvage parts. By creatively incorporating your old existing parts into the new design, you may save a lot of money.

20. Create a presence at the show – If, for whatever reason, your company decides not to exhibit at the show, consider other ways of having a presence. With proper preshow marketing, you can let your customers and prospects know that your company will still be present at the show even though you may not have a physical booth. Consider sponsoring a luncheon or seminar for attendees or renting a hospitality suite in a nearby hotel and inviting your best customers and prospects. You can also spend time walking the show floor to get an idea of what

your competitors are up to. Similarly, you can further your knowledge in the field by attending educational seminars. Remember, however, that if the show is in line with your company's objectives, it is always better to exhibit than to merely attend.

"The time to repair the roof is when the sun is shining."

– John F. Kennedy, 35th U. S. president

Chapter 17 – Lease your Exhibit

Of all the things that can be done to cut down the exhibiting budget, I have found that leasing a display is often the most confusing approach for most companies. Business owners are often confused when it comes time to find financing for their other business needs. A variety of products are out there, from government loans to bank lines of credit, to lease financing. I strongly believe that leasing is a great tool that can be used to enhance many aspects of your business, including, but not limited to, your trade show display.

You might be surprised to know that 80% of businesses in the United States lease some or all of their equipment. Whether a company specializes in computer sales, software development, heavy machine operation, or titled vehicle sales, they

---

need equipment to operate. Leasing gives the business owner the flexibility to spread out the cost of the equipment over its useful life rather than expending the entire cost up front. It is often said that the value of equipment comes from using it, not owning it. If your business has the cash to pay for the trade show display up front, you may be tempted to pay cash in order to avoid interest. But, why spend hard-earned cash, when you can spread out payments over the useful life of your exhibit? By providing you with the comprehensive leasing information in this chapter, you will gain the knowledge you need to make an educated decision about leasing.

WHY LEASING IS BETTER THAN BANK FINANCING

To begin to understand the advantages of leasing your exhibit, let's take a look at the differences between a lease and a bank loan. (see comparison chart on next page)

Loan	Lease
A loan requires the end user to invest a down payment in the equipment. The loan finances the remaining amount.	A lease requires no down payment and finances only the value of the equipment expected to be depleted during the lease term.
A loan usually requires the borrower to pledge other assets for collateral.	The leased equipment itself is usually all that is needed to secure a lease transaction.
A loan usually requires two expenditures during the first payment period; a down payment at the beginning and a loan payment at the end.	A lease requires only a lease payment at the beginning of the first payment period, which is usually much lower than the down payment.
The end user bears all the risk of equipment devaluation because of new technology.	The end user transfers all risk of obsolescence to the lessors, as there is no obligation to own equipment at end of lease.
End users may claim a tax deduction for a portion of the loan payment as interest and for depreciation, which is tied to IRS depreciation schedules.	When leases are structured as true leases, the end user may claim the entire lease payment as tax deduction. The equipment write-off is tied to the lease term, which can be shorter than IRS depreciation schedules, resulting in larger tax deductions each year.
Financial Accounting Standards require owned equipment to appear as an asset with a corresponding liability on the balance sheet.	Leased assets are expensed when the lease is an operating lease. Such assets do not appear on the balance sheet, which can improve financial ratios.
A larger portion of the financial obligation is paid in today's more expensive dollars.	More of the cash flow, especially the option to purchase the equipment, occurs later in the lease term when inflation makes dollars cheaper.

WHAT IS A LEASE?

In speaking with business owners and decision-makers, it has become readily apparent to me that the term "leasing" confuses most. Technically speaking, a lease is a transaction between a lessor and a lessee in which the lessor transfers possession and use of property for consideration (or value), but retains all right, title and interest in and to the property over a specified term, after which the property is returned to the lessor. You got that, right? Well, let's go over the above definition piece by piece. A lessee is a company that would like to obtain a piece of equipment for business use. A lessor is a leasing company that buys that piece of equipment from the vendor and allows the lessee to pay for the use of that equipment for a specified period of time. The word "property" in the above definition is very vague. But, in short, a lease can be arranged for bulldozers, buildings, computers, printing presses, trade show displays, and everything in between. The most important thing to remember is that the property should be leased for business use only. The definition above states that the property is returned to the lessor at the end of the lease. While this does happen with some quickly depreciating things such as computers, in practice, the lessee most often chooses to keep the items at the end of the lease. Lease terms vary from lease to lease. Commonly, lease terms provide that the property can be kept for one dollar, a percentage of the original price, or its fair market value at that time.

Although there are many different lease structures available, the most common is a lease in which the exhibit is yours to keep at the end of the lease, usually for a nominal price such as a dollar. The benefit with a lease is that you get the full use of your exhibit from day one and are able to pay for it over the course of a few years. Depending on these and numerous other variables that go into a lease agreement, which are all designed to give the lessee great flexibility when setting up a lease, a business may be able to take advantage of certain tax and accounting benefits that will improve the bottom line.

TAX BENEFITS OF LEASING

An often-overlooked benefit of leasing is the tax implications. If structured properly, the lease can allow your company to treat lease payments as an operating expense, and frees you from having to depreciate the equipment.

To set clear boundaries on the tax issues surrounding leases, the IRS issued a ruling in 1955 which defined what was not a true lease for tax purposes. The ruling states that if any one or more of the following conditions are present, then a transaction is not a true lease:

- Any portion of the periodic lease payment is applied to an equity position in the asset to be acquired by the lessee;

- The lessee will automatically acquire title to the property upon payment of a specified amount of "rentals" he is required to make;

- The total amount which a lessee is required to pay for a relatively short period of use constitutes an inordinately large proportion of the total sum required to be paid to secure the transfer of the title;

- The agreed "rental" payments materially exceed the current fair market value;

- The property may be acquired for a nominal purchase option in relation to the value of the property at the time the option may be exercised;

- Some portion of the periodic payment is specifically designated as interest or its equivalent.

In addition to the above conditions, there are six criteria that all have to be met in order for a lease to be considered a true lease for tax purposes. If, after professional analysis of your lease agreement, it is found that the lease is indeed a true tax lease, then this means that you, as the lessee, can treat all applicable rental payments as an operating expense. You do not have to treat the leased equipment as a liability on your books and you do not have to depreciate it over the years. The lessor is the one that technically owns the equipment, has to depreciate it over a specified period of time, and is entitled to the Investment Tax Credit. Please keep in mind, though, that the above explanation is for informational purposes only. Only your accountant or a tax professional can properly advise you on these complicated tax reporting issues.

ACCOUNTING BENEFITS OF LEASING

Another benefit that is commonly forgotten is the accounting considerations that play into your desired lease structure.

In 1976, the Financial Accounting Standards Board issued FASB statement #13. FASB 13 set forth four criteria, which classify a lease as either a capital lease or an operating lease and how each is to be treated on the financial statements of both the lessee and the lessor:

- Title to the property automatically transferred to the lessee by or at the end of the lease term;

- The lease contains a bargain purchase option;

- The lease term is equal to or greater than 75% of the estimated economic life of the leased property;

- The present value of the minimum lease payments at the beginning of the lease term is equal to or greater than 90% of the fair market value of the property, reduced by any Investment Tax Credit (ITC) retained and expected to be realized by the lessor.

A <u>capital lease</u> meets all of the above criteria and has the characteristics of a purchase agreement. Your company, as the lessee, is required to show the equipment as an asset and the stream of payments as their respective portions of short and long-term liability. Only that portion of the payment that is applicable to interest and depreciation may be expensed. The lessor must capitalize the stream of payments and may only take into income that portion of the payment that is applicable to interest.

An <u>operating lease</u>, on the other hand, meets none of

the above four criteria, and has the characteristics of a rental agreement. You, as the lessee, will not show it on your balance sheet, and will report the full periodic rental as an expense. The lessor will show the equipment as a fixed asset. All of the periodic income payments are taken into income, and depreciation and initial direct cost may be expensed. You can imagine that there is sometimes a gray line between what classifies as a capital lease versus an operating lease. For this reason, your accountant should definitely be consulted as you are making your leasing decision.

HOW CREDIT DECISIONS ARE OFTEN MADE

Once your company decides to lease an exhibit, there are different sources you can turn to. Many times, the exhibit design firm you are working with will offer a leasing package to you. This is certainly very convenient and may turn out to be a good option. The exhibit design firm, in this case, is either working with an outside leasing company to offer you this option or is working with their internal financing department to provide this valuable service to their clients. Either way, you should obtain a quote from them. But don't stop there. How do you know that you are getting the best deal on the financing? You really don't unless you take the time to shop around. There are plenty of independent leasing companies out there that want your business. They will gladly provide you with a competitive quote after reviewing some of the following factors:

- Personal credit of the owners of the company

- Time in business

- Bank and trade references

- Your industry

- Intended use of the equipment

The leasing company then makes a credit decision based on the above factors. If the dollar amount requested is over a certain threshold, which varies from lessor to lessor, then a review of company financial statements and tax returns may also be necessary. Following this process, you will receive an exact quote from the leasing company. In order to ensure that you are getting a fair price, you should obtain at least two different quotes for the exhibit that you intend to lease.

USE A BROKER'S SERVICES

Another thing your company may choose to do is utilize the services of an equipment-leasing broker. A broker is an independent company that has close relationships with many different leasing companies and can facilitate the leasing process for you. Your broker will request the above information from you and, upon reviewing it, will decide which of their funding sources is the best option for your company. Since each leasing company has its own rates, terms, and desired types of transactions, a broker will not waste time by submitting your deal to an uninterested leasing company. Even though there is a broker fee built in to your lease price when using this service, a broker will take the time to ensure that you are getting the best price and the best overall terms for your desired lease.

WHY LEASE?

In conclusion, let's review some of the advantages of leasing:

Tax Treatment – The IRS does not consider an operating lease to be a purchase, but rather a tax-deductible overhead expense. Lease payments may be deducted from income; check with your tax professional.

Balance Sheet Management – Because an operating lease is not considered a long-term debt or liability, it doesn't appear as debt on your financial statement, thus making you more attractive to traditional lenders when needed.

100 Percent Financing – Since a lease does not require a down payment, it is equivalent to 100 percent financing. You will have more money to invest in revenue-generating activities.

Immediate Write-Off – Lease payments are treated as expenses on a company's balance sheet; therefore, equipment does not have to be depreciated over five to seven years.

Flexibility – As your business grows and your needs change, you can add/upgrade at any point during the lease term through add-on or master leases. If you anticipate growth, be sure to negotiate that option when you structure your lease program.

Customized Solutions – A variety of leasing products is available. You are able to customize a program to address your needs and requirements. Some leases allow you to miss one or more payments without a penalty, an important feature for seasonal businesses.

The foregoing is a short but comprehensive overview of equipment leasing and how it can be used to maximize your trade show dollars. By consulting with your accountant and finding the best pricing available to your company, you will be well on your way to obtaining a professional display without having a large, up-front outlay.

Glossary

TERMS AND INDUSTRY LINGO YOU SHOULD KNOW

Aisle – A walkway that is intended for the movement of attendees throughout the trade show. It is best for booth staff not to stand right next to the aisle, thus blocking the exhibit.

Appointments – One of the main goals of conducting pre-show marketing is to set up appointments in the booth. Customers and prospects should have pre-determined time slots for visiting with an exhibitor.

Association – Professional associations are a great source of information when preparing for a trade show. They can assess a show's effectiveness in the specific industry, and they can recommend display manufacturers and other companies to use.

Attendees – The hundreds and thousands of people that come to trade shows to see the new products and services being offered. It is best to come to a show as an attendee before deciding whether or not to exhibit at that specific show.

Back wall Exhibit – This is the most common type of exhibit. Only one side of the exhibit is exposed to the aisle. The size of such an exhibit is usually 10x10 or 10x20, although it can sometimes be longer and a few shows still have 8x8 foot spaces.

Badge – Each attendee at a show wears a badge. Usually the badge lists basic information about the attendee, such as name, position, company, and geographic location. Different color badges are issued to buyers, vendors, students, and members of the press.

Banner – A colorful panel, usually made out of fabric or flexible vinyl that is attached to the display hung from the ceiling or supported by its own special stand. The main purpose of using banners is to convey the company's marketing message to show attendees. This can be very inexpensive.

Booth – The space in the exhibit hall where exhibitors display their products and services. The standard unit is usually 10 x10, 100 square feet of space, although many exhibiting companies choose to order several booths according to their needs, e.g. four booths to create a 20' x 20' island display.

Booth Location – Where in the show hall a booth is positioned. Larger booths are usually placed towards the center of the hall, while smaller booths can be located anywhere throughout the hall. It is important to make an educated decision when picking a location.

Booth Staff – Those people who represent the exhibitor throughout the length of the trade show. They should be professional salespeople from the company, and should be thoroughly trained to work at the show.

Branding – Having a recognizable brand name. This is not as necessary as most people think in order to be successful and attract customers. What's more important at a trade show is to concentrate on drawing a crowd of interested prospects to whom you sell your product or service. Delivering excellent customer service and support will establish your brand name. Don't put the cart before the horse, or the brand before the service.

Budget – Most companies have a limited budget set aside for exhibiting at trade shows. It is important to stick as close to that budget as possible. Following the close of the show, a thorough comparison of expected versus actual costs should be made, in order to understand exactly where and why the expected budget did not equal actual spending.

Capital Lease – It meets all of the FASB 13 criteria, and has the characteristics of a purchase agreement. The lessee is required to show the equipment as an asset and the stream of payments as their respective portions of short and long-term liability.

Common Carrier – A transportation company that moves goods for various business and personal uses. For exhibit freight, the carrier usually accepts only crated materials and consolidates the properties of several customers into one shipment bound for the same destination.

Competitors – Companies within the same industry that sell a similar product or service. At a trade show, it is likely that many competitors are exhibiting side-by-side and vying for the same customers. If you have a better booth that is easy to understand and a better crowd-pleasing presentation the competition should never be a threat.

Contractor – Provides services to the exhibitors at a trade show. The contractor is provided by the show's promotions company or, in rare cases, exhibitors are allowed to invite their own outside contractors to work on their trade show displays before and after the show. Many show contractors are union-affiliated.

Corner Booth – Such a booth is located at the end of a row. This allows for exposure on two sides of a booth, potentially attracting more visitors' attention.

Cross-Aisle Display – This type of display is usually the biggest at any trade show. It takes up both sides of an aisle, and creates an area where all show attendees will be walking down the aisle with the exhibitor's display on both sides.

Customers – Those companies that presently purchase from the exhibitor. This valued group should be marketed to heavily prior to the start of the show, and should be rewarded for setting an appointment to visit your booth.

Decision-Makers – Since fewer attendees tend to travel to trade shows from each company in recent years, it is more likely that the decision-makers are the ones who will be attending the trade show. A trade show is a great opportunity to market directly to the decision-makers.

Display Management – This is a service provided by your exhibit company. They can take over the management of your exhibit by storing it between shows, scheduling shipping to and from shows, checking it for damage after a show and handling all your paperwork. It's a great service and can remove some of the little detail tasks so you can focus on the money-making portion of the show.

Drayage – This is another word for moving heavy items, but in the trade show arena it also refers to storage. A drayage service is available at most all trade shows, for a fee. It is the process by which an exhibit is stored at the show location or at an on-site or off-site facility in the days and weeks prior to the start of the show. It also incorporates the handling of empty crates and the delivery of materials to the carrier loading area after the show.

Dress Code – All of the salespeople that represent the exhibitor at the show should dress in a similar fashion. This can be accomplished by giving out shirts with a company logo on them, or establishing a strict dress code if the salespeople are to wear their own business attire.

Entertainers – Exhibitors can hire professional entertainers to be located in their booth throughout the length of the trade show. The entertainer chosen should be one who has experience working trade shows, and has a clear understanding of the marketing opportunity that is presented. An entertainer should make sure to incorporate the exhibitor's marketing message into his or her performance. And in my opinion, they should not be dressed to look like one of your employees. What's so special about seeing a company's employee pretending to be a performer or a performer pretending to be your company rep? This can send the wrong message to your prospects if not handled skillfully. You also lose the impact of the fact that you went the extra mile and hired someone special to entertain your audience. Don't mix the two unless your employee presenter is really good and you have good reason to showcase his or her talent.

Exhibit – A collection of panels and pieces that are assembled together to create a portable image of the company. Exhibiting companies set up their exhibits at various trade shows in order to attract their desired target audience.

Exhibit Design – The process by which a display is planned out and manufactured. It is important to convey the marketing message clearly in the design of a display. There are numerous exhibit design companies out there who have the expertise needed to design an effective exhibit.

Exhibit Insurance – A company's exhibit can often be added on as a rider to the existing corporate insurance policy. Also, insurance can be bought from your freight carrier during transit. An exhibit can be an expensive investment and should be insured like any other company asset if its loss would be an issue.

Exhibit Manufacturer – The design company that puts together a trade show display. They may also offer such additional services as graphic design, storage, shipping, and repair. An exhibit manufacturer should be carefully chosen based on a thorough review of their capabilities and their understanding of the unique trade show marketing opportunities.

Exhibit Setup – The manner in which an exhibit can be set up is usually determined by whether the show is a union or non-union show. Since many trade shows are union shows, there are usually labor requirements that have to be adhered to. It is best to take on the task of supervising the union laborers as they set up your exhibit; it can save you both money and headaches.

Exhibiting – The process by which a company showcases its products and services in a setting which facilitates interaction with interested buyers.

Exhibitor Manual – A manual available for exhibitors' review prior to the show. It gives potential exhibitors an understanding of what the show management's goals are, and outlines in detail the specifics of exhibiting at the show. It contains all rules, regulations, and forms relating to a trade show. It also provides deadlines and forms for ordering services.

Fabric Display – A new technology by which images are printed on fabric rather than vinyl. Fabric is very durable, takes very little space during shipping, is a very modern look and can be cheaper than vinyl. The fabric is usually stretched on aluminum frames to create structures.

Floor Plan – A map that shows the size and locations of exhibits. It usually shows a number for each booth, and the number can be matched to a company name.

Free Advertising – Companies can get free advertising by writing and submitting effective press releases. Instead of paying thousands of dollars to run an ad in the newspaper, a company can gain exposure and credibility for free by having a press release run in a local or regional newspaper.

Freight Carrier – A shipping company that can deliver a trade show display to its designated location. Some carriers are generalists, meaning they will ship almost anything for a price. Other carriers specialize in display shipping and may be able to provide better service.

Goals – The reasons why a company chooses to exhibit their products or services. Show goals have to be specific, measurable, and relevant to the company. They have to be written down and communicated to all members of the exhibiting team.

Graphics – The various images and phrases that are used to fill up a display. They should be laminated and easily interchangeable. Graphics do not necessarily have to be bright and flashy; it is more important for the graphics to clearly convey the exhibitor's marketing message. Almost any material can be printed on today and images can be lighted from the front or back.

Hospitality Function – If appropriate for the industry, exhibitors can choose to hold an event after show hours. The main goals of such an event are to attract the best customers and prospects, and to carry the marketing message through. This is another great place for an up-close performance of magic that is very intimate.

I & D – The process by which an exhibit is installed and dismantled. This includes the proper packing up at the end of the trade show. It is important to pack the exhibit tightly with sufficient padding so that it doesn't get damaged during the shipping process, and you should take your time to document any repairs that might need to be made prior to the start of the next show.

In Line Booth – This is one of the most common types of exhibit spaces at a trade show. Only one side of the exhibit is exposed to the aisle as an in line booth. The size of such an exhibit is usually 10x10 or 10x20, although it can sometimes be longer and a few shows still have 8x8 foot spaces.

Incentives – Booth staff should be properly trained to work at the show and should be given incentives to perform at the top of their game. Setting daily goals that numerous members of the team can achieve with hard work, and rewarding the top achievers with letters of recognition and special perks can achieve this.

Island Exhibit – Island exhibits are surrounded by aisles on all four sides. This type of exhibit allows a company to market its message with a four-dimensional approach, marketing from all four sides. An island exhibit is usually a 20 x 20 space (400 square feet) or larger, and is best for companies who exhibit at a lot of trade shows throughout the year. A large island exhibit can be designed in such a way that it can be broken down into four smaller 10 x 10 exhibits, two 10 x 20 exhibits, etc.

Labor – The trade show management team provides labor for those exhibitors whose exhibits are too large to be carried in and set up by just one person. The laborers are usually members of a union. A great cost-cutting strategy is for the exhibitor to supervise the laborers instead of paying for an additional person to act as supervisor. This will also ensure that the exhibit is set up quickly and correctly.

Lead Manager – A member of the booth staff who is responsible for all of the leads collected at the show. The lead manager makes sure that there is a central collection point for all of the lead sheets that staffers complete.

Lead Processing Module – Most trade shows utilize this type of unit, which is a machine that can scan attendees' badges and collect vital information on them. Exhibitors can rent a lead processing unit from the show management. It should be used in conjunction with a lead sheet.

Lead Sheet – A form that is developed by the trade show team prior to the start of the show. Each staffer then completes this form each time they talk to a prospect. It manages information on the prospect.

Leads – Collecting qualified leads is usually the number one goal that a company has for exhibiting at a trade show. One has to be careful not to measure exhibiting success just by the number of leads collected; it is more important to see how many of those leads are converted into customers after the show ends.

Leasing – A transaction between a lessor and a lessee in which the lessor transfers possession and use of property for consideration, but retains all right, title and interest in and to the property over a specified term, after which the property is returned to the lessor.

Lifetime Warranty – Virtually all exhibit manufacturers offer a lifetime warranty on the frame of portable pop up exhibits they sell. But, one still has to be careful to choose the best quality when choosing an exhibit to buy, since shipping the exhibit back and forth to be repaired numerous times can be very expensive. It is best to go with a system that has a track record of not needing repairs.

Lighting – Lighting can be used to enhance certain areas within the exhibitor's booth. Although there is adequate lighting from the overhead lights at trade shows, it is better to use additional spotlights to highlight products, key phrases, and presentation areas within the exhibit.

Literature – The printed materials that exhibitors choose to hand out to show attendees. To be the most effective, a one-page handout should be given out, and the more expensive binders and folders should be mailed out only to qualified prospects after the show.

Logistics – Tasks surrounding the storage, transportation, set-up, and breakdown of a company's exhibit and show materials. This requires a lot of time and organization. For a fee, these tasks can be outsourced to an exhibit display company who will handle all of these tasks for the exhibitor.

Logo – A specific symbol chosen to represent a company. It is usually made up of stylized type alone or in conjunction with graphic art. A company can choose to have the logo professionally designed by a design firm, or use the services of a graphic design student in order to save money.

Magic – Magic is the best tool for attracting and holding prospects' attention at your booth. If used properly, it can also help booth staff separate the good prospects from the bad ones. The magician should incorporate the exhibitor's marketing message into their act. Your staff can even learn easy but fun close-up illusions or puzzles to share with the show attendees and prospects.

Market Research – The research that can be done prior to and following a trade show. An exhibitor can benefit by finding out such things as what the visitors' perception of their company is, if their marketing message got across like they expected, and how effective their presentation was. Market research can be conducted by staff members or can be outsourced to a marketing student who will do the work for free or a small fee.

Marketing – The process by which an exhibitor gets the word out to their customers and prospects about their upcoming exhibit. Pre-show marketing should be done weeks or months in advance, so that interested attendees can have adequate time to plan to attend the exhibitor's booth. Setting up scheduled appointments with prospects and customers is an important part of pre-show marketing.

Marketing Message – The message about the company that an exhibitor wants show attendees to walk away with. Many times, the marketing message is more important than the company name or logo, and it should be placed in the most prominent position in the exhibit. The marketing message should be clear, concise, and consistent throughout all communications with customers and prospects. No one should walk up to your booth and say, "What does your company do?"

Modular Exhibit – Exhibits constructed with interchangeable components designed to be set up in various arrangements and sizes. This is especially useful for companies who choose to design a larger exhibit. This exhibit can then be scaled down and reconfigured to be used at those trade shows where the company may not need as big a presence.

Objectives – The reasons that a company wants to exhibit at a trade show, also called goals. There are four universal trade show objectives: 1) Increasing sales 2) Getting new customers and keeping current ones 3) Introducing new products or services and 4) Establishing the company's image.

Operating Lease – It meets none of the four FASB 13 criteria, and has the characteristics of a rental agreement. The lessee will not show it on the balance sheet, and will report the full periodic rental as an expense.

Outsourcing – The process by which certain tasks are assigned to people or organizations other than the company's internal staff. Many trade show duties can be outsourced in order to save money. For example, the design of company literature can be outsourced to a college student who will design the pieces for a smaller fee than a professional graphic design firm would charge.

Overtime – The work that is performed outside of normal show working hours or on holidays. Usually, work performed on overtime is charged at 1.5 or 2 times the normal rate. When planning ahead for the setup and teardown of the exhibit, it is best to give ample time for work to be finished during normal working hours. The shows exhibitor manual should provide exhibitors a schedule that shows what hours are normal and which are charged overtime.

Peninsula Exhibit – A peninsula exhibit has three sides exposed to the traffic in the aisles. A back wall acts as the center of the exhibit. This type of exhibit is usually reserved for larger booth spaces, at least 400 square feet in size.

Post-Show Surveys – Short surveys designed to help exhibitors understand what was and was not accomplished at the trade show. They should be distributed to clients and prospects immediately following the show, and an incentive should be offered for their completion.

Postcards – Pre-show marketing should be done by mail. The most effective mailing piece is a colorful postcard. It is inexpensive, and is likely to be read because it does not have to be opened. The postcard should clearly communicate to the attendee the benefit they will get by attending the trade show and visiting the exhibitor's booth.

Pre-Made Display – If an exhibitor knows what size and type of display is best for their exhibiting needs, a pre-made display can be ordered online or through a catalog. This saves money on exhibit design services, but it only makes sense when the exhibitor is confident that they can determine their design needs on their own. Ordering interchangeable banners of various sizes can then fill up the pre-made display.

Premium – A premium is something that is given away to attendees at a trade show. It should be something special and valuable, and should only be given out to the most promising prospects and the best customers. A premium should not be handed out to just anybody that walks by an exhibitor's booth.

Presentation – Exhibitors should hold a regularly scheduled presentation in their booth. The presentation should be short, to the point, and entertaining. It should involve the crowd in some way, and should help locate the most viable prospects within the crowd.

Presenter – A professional who has experience speaking to crowds and who is knowledgeable in the product or service they will be speaking about should conduct the presentation in an exhibitor's booth. A good presenter will be able to quickly locate the most viable prospects out of a large crowd by asking certain questions.

Press – Members of the press usually walk the aisles of a trade show looking for a good story to write in their publication. Booth staff should be trained in how to best approach members of the press, and what information to share with them. Sometimes, members of the press disguise themselves as regular show attendees, so it is wise to never say anything at a trade show that should not be printed.

Press Kit – A folder or binder that contains all of an exhibiting company's marketing materials, such as press releases and product announcements. This press kit should be given out to any members of the press that stop by the booth, and should also be stocked daily in the pressroom at the trade show location.

Press Release – An article that is printed in the newspaper about an exhibiting company. An effective press release helps gain exposure in the public's eye, builds awareness of the company, and introduces new products to the public.

Press Room – Some larger trade shows have a designated area for the press. It is wise to make sure at the beginning of each show day that the pressroom is stocked with several copies of a company's press kit.

Prospects – Those among the thousands of trade show attendees who are somewhat more likely to become a company's clients. Exhibiting companies need to train their staff to pre-qualify prospects quickly by asking them a few pre-determined leading questions at the beginning of the conversation. This ensures that salespeople are using their time wisely by giving their sales presentation to the right people.

Rental – New exhibitors, and those planning on exhibiting at only one or two trade shows in the future, may be able to save money by renting a display. If, at a later date, the exhibitor wishes to purchase the display, many companies will apply the rental fee towards the cost of buying.

Return On Investment – A calculation used to determine whether a proposed investment is wise, and how well it will repay the investor. In trade show terms, it is essentially a comparison of show results to show goals. Return on investment should be calculated at pre-determined time intervals following the closing of the trade show.

Sales – Making sales directly at a trade show may be one of your goals of exhibiting. Another goal may be to make sales following the trade show, stemming from the leads collected at the show. It is important to carefully track the number and dollar amount of sales made, and the number of new customers obtained, in order to evaluate the effectiveness of exhibiting.

Shipping – The method by which a trade show display will arrive at the venue. Smaller exhibits can be shipped via common carriers such as UPS, FedEx, or DHL. Larger exhibits must be shipped with the help of a freight carrier.

Shipping Case – A container used to transport exhibit materials. It is good to use collapsible plastic shipping crates, since they are durable and take up very little space when not in use. But, some exhibit material may warrant an ATA approved shipping case for fragile or sensitive materials. Don't use a cheap case when you want your items protected.

Show Directory – The show directory is printed weeks before the show starts, and is handed out to all attendees. It contains basic show information such as a list of exhibitors, floor plan and schedule of events. The exhibitor manual provides a form, which needs to be completed and turned in on time in order for an exhibitor to be included in the directory. It may also make sense to run a small ad in the directory, thus capturing the attendees' attention.

Show Management – The management company that is responsible for putting on the trade show. This is an exhibitor's source of information prior to and during the show. Upon arriving at the show during set-up time, it is wise to get the telephone or pager number of the show manager so that no time is wasted if there is a problem with the logistics.

Signage – The message that is portrayed to show attendees by the words and phrases on an exhibit. The signs on a trade show display should clearly convey the marketing message of the exhibiting company. The lettering should be big enough to be easily read from 10-20 feet away.

Sponsors – Various suppliers and vendors who are invited to exhibit alongside the exhibiting company, thus cutting down on the cost of exhibiting.

Starbucks® Effect – This is what I call the effect of being visible in several different parts of the exhibit hall. This can be accomplished by breaking up a large booth space into several 10x10 booths, and spacing them out throughout the show floor. This strategy has the potential to capture the attention of more attendees than just one location can. It's like having a Starbucks® on every corner.

Tabletop Exhibit – These are used at trade shows where each company has only a table or a small booth to exhibit at. They can still be very effective if they are designed to properly convey the company's marketing message. It is best if such a display is used together with a matching company table cover.

Target Audience – Since it is impossible and undesirable to attract every show attendee with the display and the presentation, all of the pre- and at-show marketing efforts should be focused on attracting a desired type of attendee.

Trade Journal – The industry publication usually published by a professional association. A trade journal can be a great source of information for such things as what's hot in the industry, and which trade shows seem to be the most popular.

Trade Show – An exhibition that is organized so that companies in a specific industry or across industries can showcase and demonstrate their products and services. Trade shows are generally not open to the public and can only be attended by company representatives.

Trade Show Daily Publication – Most trade shows publish a newspaper or journal that is distributed at the beginning of each show day. This is another great marketing opportunity for exhibitors, since they can contact the publisher prior to the start of the show and submit a press release for publication.

Training – Although expensive and time-consuming, proper training of booth staff is vital to a company's exhibiting success. A trade show environment is very different from the regular working environment that most salespeople are used to, so it is not wise to assume that staffers can just transfer their skills to the show floor without any guidance.

Tradeshow Supermarket – A company that specializes in trade show exhibits and accessories with a strong focus on the complete package geared to producing successful results for their clients. They can be reached at www.capitalcityexhibits.com .

Transportation – Since most trade shows are held on a national or regional level, it is likely that the exhibiting team will have to travel by car or airplane to get to the show. To get the best deals, airline tickets should be booked months in advance. Also, the team can see if it is cheaper to fly into neighboring cities and rent a car to get to the show venue.

Union – An organization of workers formed with the purpose of protecting workers' rights and increasing bargaining power with an employer on such issues as wages, hours, and benefits. Almost all trade shows use union laborers to provide show services to exhibitors before and after the show hours.

Velcro® – The trade name for a fabric closure with two components: hook and loop. The two components stick to one another when pressed together and separate when pulled apart. This allows for repeated use. Graphics should have Hook Velcro installed on the back, so that they can be easily set up and taken down from a fabric display panel.

Vendor – A vendor is a company that sells its products or services to other companies or individuals. Trade shows are venues at which vendors across industries or from one industry come together to showcase their products and services to thousands of interested buyers.

Video Presentation – This method of attracting attendees to the booth should be used sparingly. People are more drawn to other people versus a video screen. A good use of a video presentation is to ask a prospect to watch it while they wait for the staffer to wrap up their conversation with another prospect. The video should be only a few minutes long, and informational.

Website – A company's website should be utilized in its pre-show marketing efforts. The postcards and all other pre-show communication should point potential attendees to the company's website, which should have a dedicated page for the trade show. This is an inexpensive way to promote the show to all prospects and clients.

My Gift To You –
FREE Offers and Discounts To Help Create Outrageous Profits at your next Show

BONUS #1 – $1950 VALUE
FREE – Trade Show Marketing & Design Consultation

Includes the following:
Review/Suggest – Trade Show Exhibit Design
Review/Suggest – Marketing Program (Pre-Show, During Show, Post Show)
Review & Critique – Live Presentation script or video

To activate your BONUS, fax complete information to 916-631-9988
Or activate on line at www.TSSDisplays.com/bonus

Complete information required for activation
Offer subject to withdrawal or change without notice or liability.

*Name:
*Company:
*Address:
*City: ***State:**   ***Zip:**
*Phone: **Fax:**
*Email:

Optional Book Comments:

Extra Bonus: 6 Months Free Trial subscription to "Exhibiting Results" eNewsletter, filled with quick tips and tricks of the trade.
*Limited to new subscribers and to a length of 3 months only.
I understand that I have no obligation to continue with membership; I can cancel at any time by calling Capital City Exhibits at 916-631-9900 or faxing a cancellation note to 916-631-9988.
Providing this information constitutes your permission for Troy Milligan to contact you regarding related information via mail, e-mail, fax, and phone. Your information will not be shared with any third parties. We strictly conform to anti-spam policies.

Bonus Section

My Gift To You –
FREE Offers and Discounts To Help Create Outrageous Profits at your
next Show

BONUS #2 – $937 VALUE
FREE – Milligan's Magic Marketing Program

Includes the following:
One Hour Magic Consultation (fitting magic to your product or service)
– Plus Full Reports on: Magic for Marketing, Self Working Magic for
Speakers, How To Use Magic in Sales, Advertising Magic, Milligan's
Grab The Spotlight Check List, and more.

To activate your BONUS, fax complete information to 916-631-9988
Or activate on line at www.TSSDisplays.com/bonus

*Complete information required for activation
Offer subject to withdrawal or change without notice or liability.

*Name:
*Company:
*Address:
*City: ***State:**   ***Zip:**
*Phone: **Fax:**
*Email:

Optional Book Comments:

Extra Bonus: 6 Months Free Trial subscription to "Exhibiting Results" eNewsletter,
filled with quick tips and tricks of the trade.
*Limited to new subscribers and to a length of 3 months only.
I understand that I have no obligation to continue with membership; I can cancel
at any time by calling Capital City Exhibits at 916-631-9900 or faxing a cancellation note to 916-631-9988.
Providing this information constitutes your permission for Troy Milligan to
contact you regarding related information via mail, e-mail, fax, and phone. Your
information will not be shared with any third parties. We strictly conform to anti-
spam policies.

Bonus Section

My Gift To You –
FREE Offers and Discounts To Help Create Outrageous Profits at your next Show

BONUS #3 – VALUE, PRICELESS
How To Get $1,000,000 in FREE Publicity
FREE REPORT

To activate your BONUS, fax complete information to 916-631-9988
Or activate on line at www.TSSDisplays.com/bonus

Complete information required for activation
Offer subject to withdrawal or change without notice or liability.

*Name:
*Company:
*Address:
*City: ***State:**   ***Zip:**
*Phone: **Fax:**
*Email:

Optional Book Comments:

Extra Bonus: 6 Months Free Trial subscription to "Exhibiting Results" eNewsletter, filled with quick tips and tricks of the trade.
*Limited to new subscribers and to a length of 3 months only.
I understand that I have no obligation to continue with membership; I can cancel at any time by calling Capital City Exhibits at 916-631-9900 or faxing a cancellation note to 916-631-9988.
Providing this information constitutes your permission for Troy Milligan to contact you regarding related information via mail, e-mail, fax, and phone. Your information will not be shared with any third parties. We strictly conform to anti-spam policies.

Bonus Section

My Gift To You –
FREE Offers and Discounts To Help Create Outrageous Profits at your next Show

BONUS #4 – $12 VALUE
Milligan's Trade Show Resource Directory/Guide
FREE CD

To activate your BONUS, fax complete information to 916-631-9988
Or activate on line at www.TSSDisplays.com/bonus

Complete information required for activation
Offer subject to withdrawal or change without notice or liability.

*Name:
*Company:
*Address:
*City: ***State:**   ***Zip:**
*Phone: **Fax:**
*Email:

Optional Book Comments:

Extra Bonus: 6 Months Free Trial subscription to "Exhibiting Results" eNewsletter, filled with quick tips and tricks of the trade.
*Limited to new subscribers and to a length of 3 months only.
I understand that I have no obligation to continue with membership; I can cancel at any time by calling Capital City Exhibits at 916-631-9900 or faxing a cancellation note to 916-631-9988.
Providing this information constitutes your permission for Troy Milligan to contact you regarding related information via mail, e-mail, fax, and phone. Your information will not be shared with any third parties. We strictly conform to anti-spam policies.

Bonus Section

My Gift To You –
FREE Offers and Discounts To Help Create Outrageous Profits at your
next Show

BONUS #5 – $19.99 VALUE
How To Get Dirt Cheap Premiums – Full Report
FREE REPORT

To activate your BONUS, fax complete information to 916-631-9988
Or activate on line at www.TSSDisplays.com/bonus

Complete information required for activation
Offer subject to withdrawal or change without notice or liability.

*Name:
*Company:
*Address:
*City: ***State:**   ***Zip:**
*Phone: **Fax:**
*Email:

Optional Book Comments:

Extra Bonus: 6 Months Free Trial subscription to "Exhibiting Results" eNewsletter,
filled with quick tips and tricks of the trade.
*Limited to new subscribers and to a length of 3 months only.
I understand that I have no obligation to continue with membership; I can cancel
at any time by calling Capital City Exhibits at 916-631-9900 or faxing a cancellation note to 916-631-9988.
Providing this information constitutes your permission for Troy Milligan to
contact you regarding related information via mail, e-mail, fax, and phone. Your
information will not be shared with any third parties. We strictly conform to anti-
spam policies.

My Gift To You –
FREE Offers and Discounts To Help Create Outrageous Profits at your
next Show

BONUS #6 – $240 value
PLUS 20% Discount on Printing
Full Color Printing – Sell Sheets (8.5" x 11")
PLUS
2 hours of FREE Design Time

To activate your BONUS, fax complete information to 916-631-9988
Or activate on line at www.TSSDisplays.com/bonus

Complete information required for activation
Offer subject to withdrawal or change without notice or liability.

*Name:
*Company:
*Address:
*City: ***State:**   ***Zip:**
*Phone: **Fax:**
*Email:

Optional Book Comments:

Extra Bonus: 6 Months Free Trial subscription to "Exhibiting Results" eNewsletter,
filled with quick tips and tricks of the trade.
*Limited to new subscribers and to a length of 3 months only.
I understand that I have no obligation to continue with membership; I can cancel
at any time by calling Capital City Exhibits at 916-631-9900 or faxing a cancellation note to 916-631-9988.
Providing this information constitutes your permission for Troy Milligan to
contact you regarding related information via mail, e-mail, fax, and phone. Your
information will not be shared with any third parties. We strictly conform to anti-
spam policies.

Bonus Section

My Gift To You –
FREE Offers and Discounts To Help Create Outrageous Profits at your
next Show

BONUS #7 – $120 value
Full Color Printing – Postcards
1 hour of FREE Design Time – PLUS 20% Discount on Printing

To activate your BONUS, fax complete information to 916-631-9988
Or activate on line at www.TSSDisplays.com/bonus

*Complete information required for activation
Offer subject to withdrawal or change without notice or liability.

*Name:
*Company:
*Address:
*City: ***State:**   ***Zip:**
*Phone: **Fax:**
*Email:

Optional Book Comments:

Extra Bonus: 6 Months Free Trial subscription to "Exhibiting Results" eNewsletter,
filled with quick tips and tricks of the trade.
*Limited to new subscribers and to a length of 3 months only.
I understand that I have no obligation to continue with membership; I can cancel
at any time by calling Capital City Exhibits at 916-631-9900 or faxing a cancellation note to 916-631-9988.
Providing this information constitutes your permission for Troy Milligan to
contact you regarding related information via mail, e-mail, fax, and phone. Your
information will not be shared with any third parties. We strictly conform to anti-
spam policies.

My Gift To You –
FREE Offers and Discounts To Help Create Outrageous Profits at your next Show

BONUS #8 – Up To $375 value
Royalty FREE Stock Photo Images
3 Images from our vaults – Royalty Free
May Be Used on Your Exhibit or Promotional Materials or any way you desire.

To activate your BONUS fax complete information to 916-631-9988
Or activate on line at www.TSSDisplays.com/bonus

*Complete information required for activation
Offer subject to withdrawal or change without notice or liability.

*Name:
*Company:
*Address:
*City: ***State:**   ***Zip:**
*Phone: **Fax:**
*Email:

Optional Book Comments:

Extra Bonus: 6 Months Free Trial subscription to "Exhibiting Results" eNewsletter, filled with quick tips and tricks of the trade.
*Limited to new subscribers and to a length of 3 months only.
I understand that I have no obligation to continue with membership, I can cancel at any time by calling Capital City Exhibits at 916-631-9900 or faxing a cancellation note to 916-631-9988.
Providing this information constitutes your permission for Troy Milligan to contact you regarding related information via mail, e-mail, fax, and phone. Your information will not be shared with any third parties. We strictly conform to anti-spam policies.

CPSIA information can be obtained at www.ICGtesting.com
Printed in the USA
LVOW042354100112

263297LV00002B/82/A